The Ninety-Sixth Thesis

The Ninety-Sixth Thesis

Losing Faith in the Church, Finding Faith in Christ

Brian A. Bompiani

WIPF & STOCK · Eugene, Oregon

THE NINETY-SIXTH THESIS
Losing Faith in the Church, Finding Faith in Christ

Copyright © 2020 Brian A. Bompiani. All rights reserved. Except for brief quotations in critical publications or reviews, no part of this book may be reproduced in any manner without prior written permission from the publisher. Write: Permissions, Wipf and Stock Publishers, 199 W. 8th Ave., Suite 3, Eugene, OR 97401.

Wipf & Stock
An Imprint of Wipf and Stock Publishers
199 W. 8th Ave., Suite 3
Eugene, OR 97401

www.wipfandstock.com

PAPERBACK ISBN: 978-1-7252-7715-1
HARDCOVER ISBN: 978-1-7252-7716-8
EBOOK ISBN: 978-1-7252-7717-5

Manufactured in the U.S.A.   10/13/20

In honor of the five-hundred-year anniversary of
Martin Luther's excommunication
from the Catholic Church (1521)

Contents

Preface | ix
Acknowledgments | xv
Introduction | xvii

Chapter 1
Losing Faith in the Church | 1

Chapter 2
Jesus' Miracles and the Kingdom of God | 19

Chapter 3
The Messianic Secret | 37

Chapter 4
The God Who Defies Human Wisdom | 59

Chapter 5
The Story of Abraham | 88

Conclusion | 102

Bibliography | 119

Preface

I BEGAN WRITING THIS book in 2017 after a troubling experience at church. As the months passed, I naturally began thinking of potential titles and it soon dawned on me that the evangelical teaching of tithing-to-be-blessed was not much different from the practice of selling indulgences in the days of Martin Luther. Although I knew who Martin Luther was and what he was famous for, I had only a vague idea of when he posted his grievances to the door of the church of Wittenberg. I was naturally surprised when I discovered that this happened in the year 1517, exactly five hundred years earlier from when I began writing this book. Since that time, I have worked diligently to have this book published by 2021 in honor of the five-hundred-year anniversary of Luther's excommunication from the Catholic Church. However, the more I studied Luther, the more other peculiar similarities would come to light. I was taken aback again when I discovered that Luther posted his grievances to the door of the church of Wittenberg on October 31. Why was this relevant to me? Because I was born one day later, just ten minutes after midnight on November 1. But what was really significant to me was the name of the church to which Luther posted his grievances. It was called the All Saints' Church of Wittenberg. Why was this relevant? Because November 1 is also known as All Saints' Day. Was all of this just a coincidence? Maybe, but maybe not. I will let the reader decide.

    When reading this book, it is important that the reader have some idea of why I wrote it. Since the time I lost my paternal grandfather in the year 1989, I have become increasingly more aware of how difficult life is for all of us. Like everyone else, I have lost friends and loved ones. I simply cannot fathom how some of the friends I grew up with are already gone. I sense that we all know that we are in a lot of trouble, but we do not know what to do about it. What compounds this trouble is the rapidity of life. A decade goes by so fast and the best anyone can hope for is ten of them. What is even

Preface

more troubling is the observation that the quality of life greatly diminishes with the passing of each one. When I visit nursing homes, I sometimes look around and remind myself that these are the winners. Observations such as these inevitably lead to questions about the meaning of life. Who are we? Why are we here? Is there any hope beyond this life?

For the past twenty-five years I have been looking for answers to these and other questions about God. The answers I have found are contained in this book. The good news is that I genuinely believe there is hope. Although I do not have all the answers, I cannot help but think that I am on the right track. The story of this book has a long history that began over thirty years ago. For that reason, I want to introduce this book with a short, but humorous, story that dates from that time. Although I was completely unaware of it, God was intimately and actively involved in my life moving as he so often does imperceptibly to the human senses.

I was always an ornery kid who had a habit of getting into trouble. My family considered it a great irony that I was born on All Saints' Day. On one day in the year 1987, when I was just thirteen years old, I found myself in a mess from which there was seemingly no way out. As I got ready for bed that night, all I could think about was the impending trouble that was coming my way the next morning. I did the only thing that I could. I knelt by my bed and prayed, asking God to get me out of the mess that I had made. It was a Hail Mary, but it was my only hope.

In order to understand the trouble I was in, I must turn the clock back a couple of months earlier when I received my first report card of the seventh grade. There were three F's on that report card and each F was in a major subject. I tried desperately to convince my mom that the grading system had changed since she was in school. I explained to her that F's now meant "Fantastic," D's meant "Delightful," B's meant "Bad," and A's meant "Awful." Of course, mom did not believe this. But it was not mom that I was worried about; it was dad!

Report card day was never a good day for me. I had an older brother and a younger sister, both of whom generally did well in school. I, on the other hand, had a long history of bad report cards that extended all the way back to the third grade when I received my first D! When my father returned home from work that evening, I politely allowed my brother and sister to present their report cards first. However, it was soon my turn and the following picture presented itself. My father was in the living room, seated comfortably in his favorite chair, smoking a cigarette as he watched

Preface

television. With a lot of trepidation, I walked into the room and grudgingly handed him the report card. I then tried to divert his attention away from the F's, by quickly directing his attention to the best grade on that report card, which, if I remember correctly, was a C in gym! Unfortunately, that desperate strategy did not produce the desired results. My father immediately saw the three F's and was naturally livid. He was so angry with me that he grounded me for the next nine weeks and told me that every day, right after school, I would go directly to my room and study until I brought up my grades. However, that punishment was only a small part of a much larger problem.

My teachers were naturally concerned about my poor performance too and wanted to have a conference with my father. However, my father was well-known for being a procrastinator and kept delaying the conference. Unfortunately for me he delayed it for so long that I actually received the second nine weeks report card before we had the conference from the first nine weeks. This time I did not get three F's, but five F's, again all in major subjects!

On the bus ride home that day, all I could think about was the impending punishment that was coming my way. However, as I stared at the report card, it suddenly dawned on me that the F's looked a lot like B's. After weighing the risks and calculating potential punishments, I decided it was worth a shot. I took a pencil and carefully crafted the five F's into five B's. When I got home, my father was once again seated in his favorite chair. The smell of his cigarette again filled the air. My brother and sister had just finished presenting their report cards and it was now my turn. I took a deep breath and said one last quick prayer. The show was about to start.

With much trepidation, I walked into the living room and handed my father the report card. After he took it from my hand and began examining it, there were about five to ten seconds of awkward silence. Each second felt like a minute! The longer he examined it the more likely he would notice an aberration. Finally, he spoke up and said the following words: "Brian, I am so proud of you!" He then patted himself on the back because his plan appeared to have worked. He added: "I knew that if I just made you study every day right after school you would bring up your grades." He could not have been prouder. However, the truth was that it was not his plan that worked perfectly; it was mine! Not only was I no longer grounded, but I had placated my father, who told me, for perhaps the first time, that he was proud of me. As for me, I could not believe that I had pulled this off! But

Preface

there was one significant problem. My father and I still had to go in for the conference that he had put off from the first nine weeks!

I am not sure why but, at first, I was not too worried about this conference. I imagine that I found comfort in the fact that it was still days, if not weeks, away. However, as the days began to pass, I became increasingly more concerned. Fooling my father was one thing, but fooling all my teachers was another thing. And this brings me back to the point where I started this story. The night before this conference, I did the only thing that I could. I knelt beside my bed and pleaded with God to bail me out of this mess.

When I awoke the next morning, a sickening dread enveloped me. As I got ready for school, all I could think about was that there could not possibly be a way out of this mess. My dad and I got into the truck and drove to school. I recall it being a stormy morning. Whether it really was, or whether that was just my perception of the moment, I will never know. My father parked the truck. We got out and slowly ambled toward the building. We entered the principal's office where the principal, the guidance counselor, and all my teachers were seated around a circular table. My father and my teachers exchanged introductions. Then we all sat down and the conference began.

The conference began with my teachers explaining to my father the reasons why I was doing poorly in school. They stated: "Brian does not do well on tests, is disruptive in class, rarely does homework, etc." Then my dad spoke up. Holding his head high with pride, he said: "Yes, I know Brian did not do well the first nine weeks, but I'm really proud of him because he really improved the second nine weeks!" I can still recall both my body language and the exact words that ran through my mind at that moment. Lowering my head, I prayed: "God, if you get me out of this, I will serve you the rest of my life." As hard as it may be to believe, my teachers did not question my father about this so-called "improvement." Instead, they went right back to their talking points and reiterated why they thought I was doing so poorly in school. Again, my father dismissed their concerns by explaining how proud he was of the improvement that I made the second nine weeks. Again, I lowered my head and made the same promise to God: "God, if you get me out of this, I will serve you the rest of my life." Although it may seem impossible to believe, the conference ended without anyone discovering that I changed my grades! The teachers never asked him the obvious question regarding how five F's was an improvement over three F's! As the conference was wrapping up and we were exchanging goodbyes,

Preface

I was in a state of euphoria, a feeling that must be very similar to winning the lottery. I could not believe that a thirteen-year-old boy could pull this off and deceive a roomful of so many intelligent adults.

Although this story happened over thirty years ago and although I could not possibly have been serious about this promise to serve God, in a humorous way, I ended up keeping this promise. This book is evidence of that. I eventually grew up, became a Christian, earned a PhD in Judaic, Hebraic, and Cognate Studies, and wrote this book, which is the culmination of years of research. My hope is that the information contained herein will give you something to believe in just as it has me.

Acknowledgments

I WANT TO THANK my wife, Erika, who has been with me on this journey since the beginning. She has played a major role in the completion of this book because so many of my ideas were forged in conversations that we had on long walks together. I want to thank my kids, whom I remind not to be selfish and faintly hear the voice of God saying to me, "That is what I have been trying to teach you!" I want to thank my family and especially my mom who taught her kids to pray. I want to thank my friends, especially my colleague Sam, who not only was the first to read this book, but who also shared many valuable suggestions with me. Lastly, I want to thank all of my professors. I have learned so much from all of you.

Introduction

ON OCTOBER 31, 1517, Martin Luther posted his ninety-five theses, or grievances, to the door of the All Saints' Church in Wittenberg, Germany. One of his major grievances with the Roman (Catholic) Church was its practice of selling indulgences. An indulgence was a certificate that provided the purchaser forgiveness of sins and exemption from punishment in purgatory.[1] At the beginning of the sixteenth century, the papacy was already in financial trouble when it found itself in desperate need of money for the rebuilding of St. Peter's in Rome.[2] Pope Leo X (AD 1513–1521) found a solution to this problem by selling indulgences.[3] But what was most troubling, at least in the mind of Luther, was that the promise of forgiveness of sins and exemption from punishment in purgatory could be purchased by individuals on behalf of dead relatives who could neither confess their sins nor feel contrition.[4] Preachers exhorted their listeners: "Once the coin into the coffer clings, a soul from purgatory heavenward springs!"[5] Luther rightly condemned this teaching and called it "the pious defrauding of the faithful."[6] In his view, it was nothing more than a scheme to fill the coffers of the church.[7] However, Luther's criticism of the church came at tremendous personal cost. He was eventually imprisoned,

---

1. An indulgence was basically a get-out-of-purgatory-free card. Vos writes: "In earlier days one might gain an indulgence for risking his life in fighting the infidel during the Crusades. Gradually however, financial sacrifice was accepted in lieu of physical risk" (*Church History*, 86).
2. Kittelson, *Luther the Reformer*, 104.
3. Vos, *Church History*, 86.
4. Vos, *Church History*, 86.
5. Kittelson, *Luther the Reformer*, 103–4.
6. Kittelson, *Luther the Reformer*, 104.
7. Kittelson, *Luther the Reformer*, 124.

Introduction

excommunicated from the church, and nearly sentenced to death.[8] His ninety-five theses caused a major split in the church that resulted in the Protestant Reformation.[9] However, thanks to Luther and the other reformers the Catholic Church no longer defrauds its congregations by selling indulgences. Ironically, it is now a subset of Protestant Christianity, namely evangelical churches,[10] that is defrauding the faithful.

Some evangelicals, most notably Pentecostals, promote what is called prosperity theology or the health-and-wealth gospel.[11] A hallmark of prosperity theology is the teaching that God, in the Bible, promises to bless the finances of those who give money to a minister or to his church. The origins of the prosperity gospel go back at least to the charismatic tent revivals of the 1940s and 1950s when ministers broke away from Pentecostal churches and established independent ministries.[12] Prominent among these ministers was Oral Roberts, who was one of the first to promote the teaching that giving leads to prosperity. In 1954, he told his followers that their gifts to his ministry would be paid back to them by God sevenfold.[13] Fortunately, many evangelicals regard the prosperity gospel as a perversion

---

8. The Edict of Worms declared Luther an outlaw, which meant that anyone could kill him without fear of punishment for murder (Kittelson, *Luther the Reformer*, 167).

9. Up until AD 1054 there was one universal (Catholic) church. In that year, the church split into the Roman Catholic Church and the Eastern Orthodox Church (Vos, *Church History*, 63). Luther's attack on the Roman Catholic Church's selling of indulgences led to the founding of Protestant churches. Unlike their Catholic brothers and sisters, Protestants do not follow the authority of the pope. They believe that the Bible is the final authority on all matters of the faith.

10. It is not easy to define evangelicalism, and some even question the usefulness of the term. For a brief discussion on this issue, see Collins, *Evangelical Movement*, 19–20. In this book, I follow Collins's use of the term evangelical, which refers to non-Catholic churches that share four common themes: "(1) the normative value of Scripture in the Christian life, (2) the necessity of conversion (whether or not dramatic or even remembered), (3) the cruciality of the atoning work of Christ as the sole mediator between God and humanity, and (4) the imperative of evangelism, of proclaiming the glad tidings of salvation to a lost and hurting world" (*Evangelical Movement*, 21). Unless specified otherwise, references to churches and pastors in this book always refer to evangelical churches and pastors.

11. Not all Pentecostal churches are the same. Miller and Yamamori note that "like any social movement, it has many different permutations" (*Global Pentecostalism*, 19). The largest Pentecostal denomination, at least internationally, is the Assemblies of God (Miller and Yamamori, *Global Pentecostalism*, 19).

12. Harrell, *All Things Are Possible*, 5. According to Bowler, the prosperity gospel has four main themes: "*faith, wealth, health,* and *victory*" (*Blessed*, 7).

13. Harrell, *All Things Are Possible*, 49.

Introduction

of the Christian faith. Unfortunately, however, the theological teachings of this movement are no longer limited to those Pentecostal churches that it is normally associated with, but have begun to infiltrate virtually all evangelical denominations.

Nearly all evangelical denominations today teach that Christians should tithe a tenth of their gross annual income to their local church. There is nothing wrong with denominations asking for financial support. It costs a lot of money to run churches and those who regularly attend should help support them financially. However, there is a problem with the way that tithing is taught in the church today. Because it is difficult to persuade people to give such a significant portion of their income to the church and because churches need money, many pastors have begun to use some of the same sales techniques used by prosperity preachers to persuade their congregations to tithe. The most common form of persuasion is the promise of a "special" blessing. Now the word "blessing" is a nebulous word that can mean a variety of different things depending upon the context. However, when used in evangelical churches in relation to tithing, this word is most often used to imply a financial reward for good stewardship. Thus, what many evangelical churches teach, some explicitly and others more subtly, is that God, in the Bible, promises to bless the finances of those who give a tenth of their gross annual income to the church. The result of this teaching is that there is now a very blurry line between the teachings of prosperity theology and the teachings of many evangelical churches.

The topic of tithing plays a prominent role in church sermons. Next to salvation, there are few topics that receive as much attention from pastors as tithing. Christians are very interested in this subject too. Pastors from across all evangelical denominations have touted the benefits of tithing and Christians naturally want to know how they can benefit from it. But does the Bible really teach that God blesses the finances of those who tithe, or is this just a modern-day version of indulgences and, thus, just another scheme to raise money for the church? This question is the subject of chapter 1, which explains why I am losing faith in evangelical churches.

The observation that evangelical churches are taking advantage of the faithful in the same way that the Catholic Church took advantage of them five hundred years ago might lead some to lose faith not only in the church, but also in God. Ironically, however, the opposite happened to me. The more I lost faith in the church, the more I found faith in Christ. Chapters 2 through 5 of this book explain why.

Introduction

Naturally many of us have a lot of questions about God. Who has not questioned God's existence? Who has not asked why God permits evil? Who has not asked why God allows bad things to happen? The simple solution is to conclude that God must not exist. Unfortunately, this solution is often used as an excuse to dismiss God without probing deeper for alternative answers to these questions. The fact that God encourages us to seek him suggests that there must be clues somewhere, but where? The second half of this book is about discovering the clues that will answer these and other questions about God. Although I believe that there are clues all around us, I believe that some of the most important clues are in the Bible, especially in the person of Jesus Christ. Some may legitimately ask, Jesus Christ has been studied more than anyone else in history, what more could possibly be known about him? It is the thesis of this book, particularly chapters 2 and 3, that some of the least known and most overlooked details of Jesus' life hold some of the most important clues for answering some of the most elusive questions about God.

One of the most obvious problems with the Christian faith is the glaring disconnect between the Bible and reality. The Bible records incredible stories of God's power and direct involvement in the world in the form of miracles. However, the kinds of miracles that we read about in the Bible do not seem to be happening with the same frequency and intensity today. The question is, why? Why would miracles occur in biblical times but not today? The answer to this question is found in the close relationship between Jesus' miracles and his announcement of the arrival of the kingdom of God. This relationship and its significance are the subjects of chapter 2.

Building upon the insights of the previous chapter, chapter 3 introduces readers to a little-known theme in the Gospels that is vital for understanding not only Jesus, but also God and his role in the world today. One of the reasons that people misunderstand Jesus is because they have either never heard of this theme, or they have misunderstood it. This theme is that Jesus went out of his way to keep his miracles a secret. For some reason, Jesus did not want the rank-and-file masses to discover that he was a miracle-worker. The question is, why? The answer to this question holds the clue to answering some of the most elusive questions about God, including why, despite being all-powerful, God appears to have limitations. Something is preventing God from doing all the good that he would otherwise want to do. But here is the problem. How can God have limitations? If he has limitations, then he must not be divine. However, there is one thing that could

Introduction

prevent a good, all-powerful God from doing all the good that he would otherwise want to do that would not detract at all from his omnipotence. What this is and how it can inform our understanding of God is the subject of chapter 3. At the end of this chapter, the reader will know not only what the *messianic secret* is and its significance, but also the answers to some of the most perplexing questions about God, including why he must keep his existence a secret and why he permits evil. The reader will also learn the difference between deism and theism and the reason why they are not necessarily mutually exclusive.

If the lesser-known details of Jesus' life hold important clues for understanding God and his role in the world today, then maybe there are some lesser-known details about God in the Bible that can inform our understanding of him. A careful reading of the Bible reveals a little-known but significant theme that runs through both the Old and New Testaments. This theme is that the God of the Bible reveals himself as a God who thinks and acts in defiance of human wisdom. This chapter argues that humans in their intellectual hubris are being baited into a trap and that it is the God who defies human wisdom who has set the bait. This theme and its significance are the subjects of chapter 4.

Finally, chapter 5 concludes with the story of Abraham. There are two reasons for this. Not only does it set the stage for what the entire Bible is about, but it also offers one of the most compelling reasons to believe that the Bible is indeed the word of God and that Jesus is the Christ. A conclusion follows that ties everything together.

According to the Bible, God put us on earth for a very specific reason and that is to seek him. Unfortunately, most people have never thought about the implication of this. If we are encouraged to seek God, the implication is that finding God is not going to be easy, but is going to require effort. Sadly, few people are putting forth this effort. For many, every day follows the same routine and it often seems like there is no meaning to life. Like Sisyphus, who every day pushed the rock up the hill only to have it roll back again, we too perform the same daily activities only to have to do them again the next day. But how do we seek God? Do we go out into the forest and look under rocks and behind trees? Since God is spirit (John 4:24) and cannot be seen (John 1:18), seeking and ultimately finding God must require something else, but what? It is the thesis of this book that seeking and ultimately finding God requires diligently pursuing the clues that will help us to answer the most difficult and elusive questions about God.

Introduction

    This book is not for everyone. There are a lot of people who are not going to like what I have to say. If you believe that the church is above criticism, then this book is not for you. If you are committed to a secular worldview and have already made up your mind that there is no God, then this book is not for you. This book is for those with an open-mind and those desperate to know if there is any hope beyond this life.

    Our existence is very strange. We have become so accustomed to ourselves and others like us that we barely notice that we are some kind of strange creatures. Most of us have completely forgotten that our journey began as the tiniest of seedlings. It is almost inconceivable that at one time we were tiny enough to fit neatly inside our mothers' wombs. Presently we find ourselves alive, as thinking creatures in this strange world, and no one knows for sure how we got here. Of course, the scholarly consensus is that all of this was an accident and that humans are the product of random chance and probability. But there is something very strange about this conclusion and that is that it is contradicted by one very important statistic. If we imagine eternity as a line that goes on *ad infinitum* and then imagine our lives as a tiny dot somewhere on that line, how is it possible that we now find ourselves alive in that one sliver of time when we will exist? Because eternity goes on *ad infinitum*, there can be no statistic less probable than our existence at the present time. This statistic is even more staggering when we consider that there was never a guarantee that we would ever exist in the first place. All those steps that brought us into existence—whatever they were—may never have happened. The truth is we should not be here. The fact that we are tells me that there is a reason why we are here. In order to figure out who we are and why we are here, we are going to have to do three things that do not come easily to humans.

    First, we are going to have to look for clues. This means paying attention to the world and learning from it. The fact that God encourages us to seek him suggests that there must be clues somewhere. Our job is to discover these clues.[14] Second, we are going to have to learn to listen. This means hearing not only what we want to hear, but also, and perhaps even more so, what we do not want to hear. Third, we are going to have to be authentic. This means not only being honest and open-minded to different perspectives, but also having the freedom to ask any question. Too many of

---

14. I personally believe that one of the most important clues outside of the Bible is human behavior. If history and the news have taught us anything it is that humans are capable of unimaginable evil.

Introduction

us have been taught *what* to think. What we need to do is to learn *how* to think. People say that they want authenticity. The truth is that they generally want authenticity only when it confirms what they already believe.

I suspect that this book is going to receive a lot of criticism, especially from the evangelical community, because of my position on tithing and my comparison of it with the practice of selling indulgences in Luther's day. But I would ask the evangelical community one question, when in biblical times did God ever send someone to pat the establishment on the back? It never happened. My hope is that the evangelical community will receive this book as constructive criticism. It is not meant to destroy the church, but to make it better. I hope that the criticism does not override the positive message of this book, and that is that there is a God whose role in the world can be discerned by those who diligently seek him. This book is written for those who would like to seek God but are limited by the constraints of time and chance or perhaps do not know where to start. Most people have at least a vague conception of God. What I want to do in this book is take that vague conception and bring it into sharper focus. The more questions that we can answer about God, the better we can understand him and his role in the world, as well as our role in it. But first it is necessary to bring an indictment against the evangelical movement.

Chapter 1

Losing Faith in the Church

A FEW YEARS AGO, a local car repair shop had a large banner over their garage door that advertised Wednesday as "Ladies Day." Every Wednesday ladies would get a dollar off their already low-priced oil change. Instead of paying $19.99, they would pay only $18.99. On the surface, this seems like an act of goodwill. After all, it seems like this garage is trying to save ladies a little money. But is this garage really trying to save them a little money, or is something else going on here?

An immediate red flag that something unethical is going on here derives from the fact that garages make very little, if any, money off a twenty-dollar oil change. It costs more than that for someone to change the oil him or herself. The question that must be asked is, how can any garage afford to perform oil changes that barely cover the costs of parts and labor? The truth is that the cheap oil change is bait and those who show up to have their oil changed have taken the bait. The dollar savings is not evidence that the garage cares about women, but rather an attempt to bait into their garage a segment of society that generally knows little about cars for no other reason than to take advantage of them. The unsuspecting customer who thinks she is getting a deal on an oil change ends up with a litany of other things that the garage found wrong with the car while performing the oil change and ultimately a much more expensive bill. While it probably surprises no one that some businesses take advantage of customers like this, it is alarming to discover that the church, the most sacred and divine of all institutions, also takes advantage of people with its own form of bait.

The Ninety-Sixth Thesis

Few topics receive more attention from evangelical churches than tithing.[1] Tithing is the practice of giving 10 percent of one's gross annual income to the local church. There is nothing wrong with churches asking those who attend to tithe. Churches are businesses and it costs a lot of money to support them. However, there is a problem with the way that tithing is taught in evangelical churches today. Because it is difficult to get people to give such a significant amount of their income to the church, many churches have sweetened the pot with the promise that God will bless the finances of those who tithe to their local church. Thus, what many evangelical churches teach is that the more money individuals give to their local church, the more money they will get back in return, a teaching that is in total harmony with prosperity theology.[2]

The second chapter of Hood's book *Take God at His Word: Experience the Power of Giving* bears a title that succinctly summarizes the view of many evangelical churches with respect to giving: "I Want You to Tithe So I Can Reward You."[3] He explains: "This chapter focuses on the incredible blessings that God has promised once we decide to give at least a tenth of our income back to God. Giving a tenth, also called 'tithing,' should actually be a starting point in our giving. The Bible clearly teaches that the Lord is looking to bless us as a result of our important step of faith."[4]

---

1. For those who want a more comprehensive study of this topic, I recommend Russell Kelly's book *Should the Church Teach Tithing?*

2. When someone makes an accusation like this against a movement that is as broad and as nebulous as the evangelical movement is, it is only natural to expect the accused to say, "Surely not I?" Very few would admit to preaching the prosperity gospel. This is clear from the fact that even those who explicitly teach tithing-to-be-blessed almost always add a disclaimer somewhere that they are not teaching prosperity theology. So the question becomes, what percentage of evangelical churches teach prosperity? A recent survey done by Nashville-based LifeWay Research suggests that four in ten evangelicals are taught the prosperity gospel. I personally believe that the number is much higher and there are indications of that in this same survey. According to LifeWay, nearly seventy percent agree with the statement "God wants me to prosper financially." "Among those who attend [church] at least once a week, 71 percent say God wants them to prosper financially." "Churchgoers who have evangelical beliefs (75%) are more likely to agree God wants them to prosper than those without evangelical beliefs (63%)." "Pentecostal and Assemblies of God (80%), Baptist (74%), nondenominational (67%) and Methodist churchgoers (65%) are among the most likely to agree." Smietana, "Prosperity Gospel," July 31, 2018.

3. Hood, *Take God at His Word*, 23.

4. Hood, *Take God at His Word*, 23.

In his book *The Treasure Principle*, Alcorn writes: "The more you give, the more comes back to you, because God is the greatest giver in the universe, and He won't let you outgive Him."[5] Youssef is another writer who teaches that the secret to getting is through giving.[6] He writes that people "are always thinking about how they can get more and more and more—and they do not understand that the secret for positive living is *getting by giving*."[7] A few paragraphs later, he explains: "If we give sacrificially, God will give generously to us. Giving is the secret to activating God's amazing give-back program. It's impossible to outgive God."[8] An unfortunate result of this teaching is that many are giving on Sunday with the expectation that an unexpected check might arrive in the mail Monday through Friday![9] But is this really what the Bible teaches? Will Christians who tithe really receive more money in return?

In many evangelical churches tithing has become *the* litmus test of spiritual maturity. Those who tithe are regarded with higher esteem in the church and are treated as if they have accomplished the spiritual equivalent of having climbed Mt. Everest or having been inducted into the Hall of Fame. Those who do not tithe are often treated like second-class citizens who are not "good" Christians. But is it really fair to judge someone's spiritual growth on the basis of how much money they give to the church? Would Jesus have done this? Unfortunately, many pastors seem to believe that this is acceptable.

A few years ago, I had the privilege of attending a Nazarene church that had a great pastor with a sincere heart. One evidence of his sincerity was that he never wanted to know who gave what to the church. However, when other pastors in his denomination heard this, many of them criticized him because, in their view, pastors have a right to know who gives what to the church because tithing is a measure of spiritual growth! In other words, they believed they could discern who was growing spiritually by looking at how much money people gave to the church.

5. Alcorn, *Treasure Principle*, 71.
6. Youssef, *15 Secrets to a Wonderful Life*, 145.
7. Youssef, *15 Secrets to a Wonderful Life*, 147.
8. Youssef, *15 Secrets to a Wonderful Life*, 148.
9. Youssef writes: "And you know what will happen if you are a cheerful, hilarious giver? The very thing you need most will arrive from a completely unexpected source. And you'll say, 'Bless the Lord, more money to give to God!' And as you keep thanking God and giving back to Him, you'll find money and resources popping up here and there, all over the place" (*15 Secrets to a Wonderful Life*, 168).

The Ninety-Sixth Thesis

Over the years I have attended a number of evangelical churches that span a broad spectrum of denominations and the one thing that so many of them have in common is the teaching, some explicitly and others more subtly, that tithing leads to some form of prosperity.

Some pastors shout platitudes to persuade their congregations to tithe. One of the most common platitudes is the well-known and overused: "You can't out give God!"[10] The implication is clear: the more money one gives to the church, the more money one gets back in return! Other pastors use urban legends to make their appeal and tell unsubstantiated stories about individuals who started to tithe and a week or so later received unexpected checks in the mail.[11] Other pastors use the threat of financial ruin to frighten their congregations to tithe. They not only teach that God blesses the finances of those who tithe, but that he curses the finances of those who do not![12] In her book *Blessed*, Bowler writes about a pastor who taught that non-tithers' households may be cursed, their vehicles might break down, and their bills might not get paid![13] I recently heard an example similar to this at a Nazarene church I attended. The pastor said that a young couple came to him to discuss their financial problems. He then said that the first thing he asks anyone who comes to him with financial difficulties is: "Are you tithing?" Why does he ask this question? Because, in his view, they would not be having financial problems if they were tithing!

To most people 10 percent of their total income is a real sacrifice. But for some pastors even 10 percent is not enough! In their view, 10 percent

---

10. This example offers a perfect illustration of one of the problems with all false teaching: there is often a kernel of truth to it. It is of course true that no one could ever give more to God than he has already given to them, but the Bible does not teach that the more money one gives to the church, the more one can expect in return.

11. Hood writes about a Christian who started tithing and his business suddenly quadrupled (Hood, *Take God at His Word*, 29). While that may be true, it is important to remember that correlation does not necessarily imply causation. Just because two events happen at the same time does not mean that the one caused the other. Because pastors speak to hundreds and thousands of people, it should not surprise anyone that some of those who tithe have success stories. The question is, is the success related to tithing, or is it coincidental?

12. See Hood, *Take God at His Word*, 32. The threat of financial ruin is nothing new and goes back to at least the tent revivals of the late 1940s and early 1950s. In 1956, one of the criticisms of the General Presbytery of the Assemblies of God of the independent ministers was questionable fund-raising methods, including "threats of judgment or disaster upon those who do not respond to financial appeals" (Harrell, *All Things Are Possible*, 108–9).

13. Bowler, *Blessed*, 235–36.

should be the starting point of giving. Alcorn writes: "Tithing isn't the ceiling of giving; it's the floor. It's not the finish line of giving; it's just the starting blocks."[14] This is also the perspective of Hood, who writes: "Giving a tenth, also called 'tithing,' should actually be a starting point in our giving."[15] I once heard a pastor call church members who tithe but give nothing more stingy! I heard another pastor tell his congregation: "If you are not with us financially, then get out!" Few who regularly attend an evangelical church would find any of these comments incredible.

Because evangelicals consider tithing as a key to financial success, many pastors encourage their congregations to tithe to their church before paying their own bills! In his book *The Money Challenge*, Rainer writes: "Giving is not about providing the leftovers. Giving is a prioritized act that often requires sacrifice. Before bills? Yes. Before debt? Yes. Before savings? Yes."[16] But what about those who genuinely cannot afford to give, let alone tithe? Apparently, there are no such people. In the view of many pastors, everyone can afford to tithe and no one can afford *not* to tithe![17] Why can no one afford not to tithe? Because tithing leads to prosperity. Alcorn explains: "Ironically, many people can't afford to give precisely *because* they're not giving (Haggai 1:9–11). If we pay our debt to God first, then we will incur His blessing to help us pay our debts to men. But when we rob God to pay men, we rob ourselves of God's blessing. No wonder we don't have enough. It's a vicious cycle, and it takes obedient faith to break out of it."[18]

When I first became a Christian approximately twenty-five years ago, the pastor of the Wesleyan church I attended taught that tithing leads to God's blessing. When he preached on the topic of tithing, he said that people always wanted to know whether they should tithe on their net or gross income. He then said that he always responds to this question with the same answer: "That depends, how big of a blessing do you want?" Naturally I wanted God to bless my finances so I too began to tithe. However, instead of receiving a financial blessing, I found myself spiraling further into debt. Being fresh out of high school, I did not make a lot of money. After paying

---

14. Alcorn, *Treasure Principle*, 62.
15. Hood, *Take God at His Word*, 23.
16. Rainer, *Money Challenge*, 30.
17. Hood, *Take God at His Word*, 38. The argument that people cannot afford not to tithe has been around for a long time. In his 1926 book, *The Call to Christian Stewardship*, Julius E. Crawford, a southern Methodist, concluded that those "who wanted to be successful could not afford not to tithe" (Hudnut-Beumler, *Almighty's Dollar*, 72).
18. Alcorn, *Treasure Principle*, 64.

bills, there was very little money left over. However, I still remained faithful and tithed even if it meant that I had to withdraw money from a credit card to do it! As I continued to struggle financially, I went to my pastor and explained my situation. He concluded that I must have done something wrong. Looking back today, I now know he was correct. I was doing something wrong; I was listening to him!

My story is by no means unique. There are many websites where Christians express their frustration with tithing. They have been taught that tithing leads to prosperity, however, they tithe and yet remain broke.[19] Some pastors like to discredit or dismiss their stories by suggesting that they must be doing something wrong. But are all these people really doing something wrong or, perhaps more likely, is this teaching wrong?

Like the prosperity teachers, evangelical pastors and church leaders support their teaching of tithing-to-be-blessed with proof texts from the Bible that *appear* to support their teaching. However, even before examining those scriptures, there are a number of reasons to be immediately suspicious of the legitimacy of this teaching.

First, does it really make sense that God would teach us to give only to get more in return? This is a very immature form of giving that appeals only to our human desires. That is the first clue that this teaching does not derive from God.

Second, if God blesses the finances of those who tithe, why then are there so many Christians who tithe and yet remain broke?

Third, if tithing is one of the keys to financial success, does it not seem strange that the financial experts of the world have failed to make this connection? Surely if there were any truth to this teaching it would not have escaped their notice.

However, even if we were to lay these three objections aside, the most compelling reason to reject this teaching would still remain. If God blesses the finances of those who tithe, why then were so many of the men and women we read about in the Bible poor? For example, both John the Baptist

---

19. Of course, there are people who testify that they have been blessed financially as a result of tithing. Miller and Yamamori have an interesting thought on this. They write: "Presumably one might ask whether the act of tithing resulted directly in an individual's prosperity or whether leading a disciplined life enabled that individual to have surplus capital, from which he or she could pay tithes. Correlation is often mistaken for causation, even among social scientists" (*Global Pentecostalism*, 176). Even Hood admits that "People who are committed to tithing evaluate their spending habits more closely" (*Take God at His Word*, 31).

and the Apostle Paul—two of God's most faithful servants—were poor in this life (Matt 3:4; 2 Cor 6:10). If God did not bless their finances, why should modern Christians think that he wants to bless them financially? Similarly, Jesus praised the poor old woman for giving her only two coins to the temple treasury (Mark 12:41–44). She gave more than a tithe and yet she was still poor. If God blesses the finances of those who tithe, why then was this woman poor in the first place? Where was her blessing? Where was her financial reward for good stewardship? Clearly there is a disconnect between the teachings of the Bible and the teachings of evangelical churches.

Evangelical leaders like to legitimize their teaching of tithing-to-be-blessed by appealing to Old Testament scriptures that *appear* to support their teaching. The passage of scripture most often appealed to is Mal 3:7–12. In this passage God says:

> "Ever since the time of your forefathers you have turned away from my decrees and have not kept them. Return to me, and I will return to you," says the LORD Almighty. "But you ask, 'How are we to return?' Will a man rob God? Yet you rob me. But you ask, 'How do we rob you?' In tithes and offerings. You are under a curse—the whole nation of you—because you are robbing me. Bring the whole tithe into the storehouse, that there may be food in my house. Test me in this," says the LORD Almighty, "and see if I will not throw open the floodgates of heaven and pour out so much blessing that you will not have room enough for it. I will prevent pests from devouring your crops, and the vines in your fields will not cast their fruit," says the LORD Almighty. "Then all the nations will call you blessed, for yours will be a delightful land," says the LORD Almighty.

A casual reading of this passage may seem to support the teaching that God blesses the finances of those who tithe. However, when reading the Bible it is important to know what the whole Bible says about a particular topic rather than selecting one text to support a particular position.[20] Unfortunately, it is this lack of general knowledge of the entire Bible that allows those who are most vulnerable—such as new Christians and those

---

20. For example, if one were unaware of Paul's New Testament letters that teach that Christians are under no obligation to be circumcised, one could easily reach the opposite conclusion by reading Old Testament passages that promote circumcision. All passages must be read with their immediate and remote contexts in mind (the context of the Bible as a whole). In Old Testament times, all Jews were required to be circumcised. Christians, on the other hand, are under no obligation to be circumcised (Gal 5:1–15).

who don't know a lot about the Bible—to be taken advantage of by false teachings.[21] Although a superficial reading of Malachi 3 may *appear* to support the teaching that tithing leads to prosperity, there are at least two major problems with this interpretation.

First, there is a tendency in the church today, particularly in the West, of thinking individually. People who regularly attend church have been taught to think about how God can bless them personally. An example of this is the popular book *The Prayer of Jabez*, which encourages Christians to pray selfishly and ask God to bless them first![22] But in the Old Testament, when the Bible speaks of blessing, the blessing is most often corporate in nature and thus a blessing for the nation of Israel as a whole. Malachi 3 is a perfect example of this.

Ancient Israel was an agrarian society that depended on rain for agriculture. Notice v. 11, which reads, "I will prevent pests from devouring your crops, and the vines in your fields will not cast their fruit," says the LORD Almighty. The point of Malachi 3 is not that God will bless the finances of every individual who tithes to his or her local church, but that he will bless the nation of Israel as a whole with an abundance of crops and rain.[23] It is a gross misinterpretation of this passage to teach that God is going to financially reward every individual who tithes to his or her local church. Churches did not even exist when Malachi wrote this passage!

The second, and more significant, problem with using Malachi 3 to teach that God blesses the finances of those who tithe is that it belongs to the Old Testament. The Old Testament literally means the *Old* Covenant (or agreement). The Old Testament is God's covenant with ancient Israel, not God's covenant with the church. Christians live under a New Covenant (or New Testament) inaugurated with the death and resurrection of Christ. The New Covenant (or New Testament) repeatedly states that Christians do not live under the authority of Old Testament law.

---

21. Jones and Woodbridge make a similar observation. They write: "Many followers of the prosperity gospel have little knowledge of biblical doctrine. Therefore, they are ripe for accepting the distorted teachings of prosperity preachers. This is especially true given the Christian veneer of the prosperity message, which makes it attractive to listeners who may lack theological discernment" (*Health, Wealth & Happiness*, 19).

22. Wilkinson, *Prayer of Jabez*, 18–19.

23. The corporate notion of this passage is most clearly articulated in v. 9 which states that the curse is directed toward "the whole nation of you." Another indication of this are the personal pronouns in the phrases "your crops" and "your fields" which are plural in Hebrew (Mal 3:11).

> For we maintain that a man is justified by faith *apart from observing the law*. (Rom 3:28)
>
> For sin shall not be your master, *because you are not under law*, but under grace. (Rom 6:14)
>
> But now, by dying to what once bound us, *we have been released from the law* so that we serve in the new way of the Spirit, and not in the old way of the written code. (Rom 7:6)
>
> We who are Jews by birth and not "Gentile sinners" know that *a man is not justified by observing the law*, but by faith in Jesus Christ. So we, too, have put our faith in Christ Jesus that we may be justified by faith in Christ and *not by observing the law*, because *by observing the law no one will be justified*. (Gal 2:15-16)[24]

Since Christians do not live under Old Testament law, Malachi 3 is completely irrelevant to Christians; it does not apply to them in the same manner that it did to ancient Israel. Unfortunately, many pastors and church leaders are not even aware of this basic New Testament teaching. The Old Testament is still important for Christians in that it teaches who God is and how he worked in the past to bring about salvation. However, Christians are under no obligation to obey the Old Testament laws because we do not live under Old Testament law, but under grace (Rom 6:14).

Unlike Jews who lived under Old Testament law and were required to strictly obey every Old Testament commandment, Christians are required to obey Jesus' two simple commands to love God and to love neighbor (Matt 22:37-39). This is important because some pastors and church leaders try to make folly of the argument that Old Testament law does not apply to Christians by arguing that if Christians are not required to observe Old Testament law then Christians would be allowed to commit adultery and murder. What they do not understand is that Jesus' command to love God and neighbor eliminates the need for Old Testament law. If one really loves God and neighbor, he would never even think of worshiping idols, stealing, committing adultery or murder. Thus, love naturally leads Christians to keep the

---

24. "Before this faith came, we were held prisoners by the law, locked up until faith should be revealed. So the law was put in charge to lead us to Christ that we might be justified by faith. Now that faith has come, *we are no longer under the supervision of the law*" (Gal 3:23-25). "By calling this covenant 'new,' he has made the first one obsolete; and what is obsolete and aging will soon disappear" (Heb 8:13). See also Gal 2:19, Eph 2:15, et al.

The Ninety-Sixth Thesis

moral laws of the Old Testament which are relational. But the ceremonial laws of the Old Testament, including tithing, do not apply to the church!

That tithing is not incumbent upon Christians is also clear from the decision of the first church council, recorded in Acts 15. One of the first problems that arose in the early church was the question regarding how Christians should live in relation to Old Testament law. It is important to remember that the early church was largely a Jewish movement. The early Christians were Jews and the Old Testament was the Bible of the early church. The New Testament had not yet been written. Naturally, the first Christians wanted to know if they were required to keep the Old Testament laws, as the Jews were. Some early Christians who belonged to the party of the Pharisees argued that Gentiles must be circumcised and required to obey the law of Moses.[25] However, the first council of the early church reached the opposite conclusion. Their decision is recorded in the book of Acts 15:6–11, 27–29:

> The apostles and elders met to consider this question. After much discussion, Peter got up and addressed them: "Brothers, you know that some time ago God made a choice among you that the Gentiles might hear from my lips the message of the gospel and believe. God, who knows the heart, showed that he accepted them by giving the Holy Spirit to them, just as he did to us. He made no distinction between us and them, for he purified their hearts by faith. Now then, why do you try to test God by putting on the necks of the disciples a yoke that neither we nor our fathers have been able to bear? No! We believe it is through the grace of our Lord Jesus that we are saved, just as they are.
>
> "Therefore we are sending Judas and Silas to confirm by word of mouth what we are writing. It seemed good to the Holy Spirit and to us not to burden you with anything beyond the following requirements: You are to abstain from food sacrificed to idols, from blood, from the meat of strangled animals and from sexual immorality. You will do well to avoid these things. Farewell."

---

25. God made a covenant with Abram that he and all his descendants must be circumcised in the flesh (Gen 17:9–14). This covenant was to be an "everlasting" covenant (Gen 17:13). Thus, in order to be part of the family of God in Old Testament times one had to be circumcised. Naturally, many of the Jews who became Christians in New Testament times wanted to know if Christians were required to be circumcised.

If tithing or any other Old Testament law were incumbent upon the early Christians, the first church council would have listed it here. But they did not! Tithing is completely absent from this list.[26]

Because Christians have been set free from Old Testament law, tithing is no more incumbent upon the church than any of the other Old Testament ceremonial laws.[27] How is it possible for churches and pastors to treat all the other Old Testament laws—such as circumcision, the dietary laws, animal sacrifices, etc.—as irrelevant, and yet argue that Christians are somehow still obliged to obey just this one law from the Old Testament? Is it merely a coincidence that this is the one law that benefits them financially?

Naturally some pastors and church leaders do not like the argument that tithing does not apply to Christians on the grounds that it is an Old Testament law. Therefore, they have developed other, more sophisticated, arguments to circumvent what is otherwise a clear teaching of scripture. They point out that although tithing eventually became part of Old Testament law at the time of Moses, it was actually practiced much earlier than the giving of the law at Sinai, such as when Abram tithed to Melchizedek (Gen 14:20) and when Jacob vowed to give a tenth to God (Gen 28:22). Their argument is that since the patriarchs (Abram and Jacob) practiced tithing hundreds of years before the giving of the law at the time of Moses, tithing is a "universal" law that is incumbent upon all believers throughout all ages, including Christians. However, there are several problems with this argument.

First, could not the opponents of Paul have used this same argument to support their belief that Christians should be circumcised? Although circumcision was a Jewish custom that eventually became part of Old Testament law (Lev 12:2–3), it was actually practiced hundreds of years earlier during the time of Abram (Gen 17:9–14).[28] If one is going to argue that Christians should tithe because Abram tithed, then one would have to argue that Christians should also be circumcised, since Abram also practiced circumcision (Gen 17:23–27). But Paul's New Testament letters repeatedly state that Christians are under no obligation to be circumcised (Gal 5:1–6).

---

26. Again, they did not have to list all the moral laws of the Old Testament because Jesus' command to love God and neighbor naturally leads Christians to keep those laws.

27. Col 2:14 talks about Christ "having canceled the written code, with its regulations, that was against us and that stood opposed to us; he took it away, nailing it to the cross."

28. In his book *Should the Church Teach Tithing?*, Kelly notes two other laws, the Sabbath and unclean foods, that are not obligatory for Christians even though they preceded the giving of the law and were later included in it (*Should the Church Teach Tithing?*, 28–29).

The Ninety-Sixth Thesis

If Christians are not required to be circumcised, even though circumcision preceded the giving of the law at the time of Moses, then the argument that Christians are required to tithe because tithing preceded the giving of the law is baseless.

Second, the tithing practiced by Abram in Genesis 14 is very different from the tithing that is taught in evangelical churches. In Genesis 14, Abram gave a priestly king a *one-time* gift from the spoils of *one* particular battle. A one-time gift from the spoils of battle is hardly comparable to the concept of tithing taught in churches today, which requires that one regularly offer a tenth of one's gross income to the church. Are we to believe that Abram regularly met with Melchizedek to pay tithes? Not only is there no indication of that in the narrative, but Melchizedek is never mentioned again in Genesis. The logical inference is that this was nothing more than a onetime gift from the spoils of war.

Third, when Christians tithe, they give a tenth of their *own* income to God. That is very different from the situation in Genesis 14, where Abram gave Melchizedek a tenth of the spoils of war, not a tenth of his own property.

In summary, not only does the Old Testament not teach that God blesses the finances of those who tithe, it does not even teach that Christians are under any obligation to tithe! Christians do not live under Old Testament law, but under grace (Rom 6:14). If one wants to support tithing on the basis of scripture then, that support must come from the New Testament. But, as some may already suspect, there is a reason why those who push tithing consistently appeal to Old Testament scriptures.

Because churches place so much emphasis on the importance of tithing, it may surprise some to discover that *there is not a single command to tithe anywhere in the New Testament*. In fact, tithing is mentioned in only three passages in the entire New Testament.[29] Although Paul wrote much of the New Testament, he never mentions the topic of tithing.[30] The question that every Christian should ask is, how can a topic that gets so little attention in the New Testament play such a prominent role in church

---

29. Matt 23:23 (and its parallel in Luke 11:42), Luke 18:12, and Heb 7:1–10.

30. Pastors like to use Paul's words in 1 Cor 16:2 as an exhortation to collect money for the church. This verse reads: "On the first day of every week, each one of you should set aside a sum of money in keeping with his income, saving it up, so that when I come no collections will have to be made." However, if one carefully reads 1 Corinthians and Paul's other letters it becomes clear that he is not collecting money for a building, but rather for the poor in Jerusalem (1 Cor 16:1–4; 2 Cor 8:1—9:13; Rom 15:14–32).

sermons? The answer is obvious. Churches have become businesses and, like any business, must raise money to survive.

An examination of the three New Testament passages that mention tithing reveals even more clearly why these passages are disregarded in favor of Old Testament passages: not one of them either commands or even encourages Christians to tithe! In Luke 18:12 Jesus tells a parable about a self-righteous Pharisee who thought that his obedience to Old Testament law, including tithing, gave him better standing before God than the repentant tax collector. In Heb 7:1–10 tithing is mentioned several times in a passage that highlights the superiority of Jesus' priesthood over the Old Testament priesthood of Levi. It mentions tithing only as a regulation of the past required by the law.[31] "Now *the law requires* the descendants of Levi who become priests to collect a tenth from the people" (Heb 7:5).[32] The only other New Testament passage that mentions tithing is Matt 23:23 and its parallel in Luke 11:42. Although a superficial reading of this passage has led some to conclude that Jesus taught that Christians should tithe,[33] a closer examination of it reveals otherwise.

In Matt 23:23 Jesus says: "Woe to you, teachers of the law and Pharisees, you hypocrites! You give a tenth of your spices—mint, dill and cumin. But you have neglected the more important matters of the law—justice, mercy and faithfulness. You should have practiced the latter, without neglecting the former." Here Jesus criticized the Pharisees for meticulously observing less important Old Testament laws, such as tithing, while neglecting other laws that were deemed more important. Jesus said that they were right to tithe, but they should not have neglected the more important laws of justice, mercy, and faithfulness. Although on the surface this sounds like an endorsement of tithing, it must be remembered that Jesus and the Pharisees he was addressing in this passage were all Jews who lived under

---

31. The point of this passage is that Jesus' priesthood is superior to that of Levi, and one evidence of that is that Abraham, the progenitor of Levi, paid tithes to Melchizedek. Again, there is no command to tithe in this passage. Rather it is a description of a historical event that happened in the past that is highlighted to prove the superiority of Jesus' priesthood.

32. This passage highlights another reason to reject the church's teaching of tithing and that is that only Levites were permitted to collect tithes! The reason for this is that they were the only one of the twelve tribes of Israel that did not receive any land as an inheritance (Deut 12:12; 14:27, 29; 18:1–2; Josh 13:14, 33; 14:3; 18:7). The tithe was literally a tax that compensated them for their lack of land.

33. Alcorn, *Treasure Principle*, 60. Ramsey must have had this passage in mind when he wrote: "The affirmation of the tithe and the command to obey it appears throughout both the Old and New Testaments" (*Complete Guide to Money*, 315).

The Ninety-Sixth Thesis

Old Testament law. The Old Testament law became obsolete *only after Jesus' death and resurrection*. Thus, it is no surprise that Jesus endorsed tithing in this passage. He was addressing Jews who lived under the law, not Christians who do not live under Old Testament law. Jesus' Jewish contemporaries were obligated to strictly observe not only the law of tithing, but also all of the other Old Testament laws. Thus, the argument that Christians should tithe on the basis of Jesus' words in Matt 23:23 completely falls apart upon closer scrutiny.

When reading the New Testament, we must make a distinction then between the words that Jesus said that applied only to his Jewish contemporaries who lived under the law and those words that he spoke that are timeless and apply universally to everyone throughout all ages. Those things that Jesus said to his contemporaries with regard to the law do not apply to Christians today. Those who argue that Christians should tithe on the basis of Jesus' words in Matt 23:23 betray a certain level of hypocrisy when they do not maintain other aspects of the law endorsed by Jesus. For example, Jesus not only endorsed tithing, but also the offering of animal sacrifices at the temple (Matt 5:23–24). Should Christians reinstate animal sacrifices? Of course not! And no educated Christian would ever make such an argument, because they would know that we do not live under Old Testament law, but under grace (Rom 6:14).

Similarly, when the rich young ruler asked Jesus what he must do to inherit eternal life, Jesus responded by telling him to obey the Ten Commandments (Matt 19:17). Yet, few Christians would agree that the way to heaven is by keeping the Ten Commandments. Why? Because, again, Jesus was speaking to Jews who lived under the law. Thus, Jesus' endorsement of tithing in Matt 23:23 is no more relevant to Christians than his endorsement of the sacrificial system or his endorsement of the law as the way to receive eternal life (Matt 19:16–19). When Jesus spoke to his contemporaries about matters pertaining to Jewish law, he was speaking to Jews who lived under Old Testament law, not to Christians who do not live under Old Testament law.

It should be clear by now that not only does the New Testament not teach that Christians who tithe will be blessed financially, it does not even teach that Christians are obligated to tithe. When pressed on these arguments, many pastors backpedal and argue that the blessings associated with tithing may not be financial, but may come in some other form.[34] However,

---

34. In the writings of those who teach tithing-to-be-blessed there is usually a disclaimer

the argument that people who tithe may be blessed in some other way does not correspond with the Bible either.

Who in the Bible really had what we would consider a blessed life here on earth? With few exceptions, the men and women we read about in the Bible were not only poor, but their lives were extremely difficult. Jeremiah was beaten (Jer 20:2) and thrown into prison (Jer 37:16). The Apostle Paul was not only beaten and imprisoned, but also stoned and left for dead (Acts 14:19). If God blesses those who tithe, where were their blessings? Where was their promise of a blessed life? Unfortunately, if Jeremiah or Paul were to walk into some of our pastors' offices today with their résumés, some pastors would immediately conclude that they must not be tithing! However, their problems did not derive from the fact that they were not tithing. Their problems derived from the fact that they lived in the same fallen world in which we live. The truth is that God promises no one a blessed life here on earth; it is completely irrelevant whether they tithe to their local church or not.

The evangelical teaching of tithing-to-be-blessed is systemic of a much deeper and more significant problem within the church today and that is that the gospel that many evangelical churches are preaching is a false gospel that more closely resembles the American dream than the gospel of Jesus Christ. I will discuss this in more detail in the conclusion of this book. For now, it is sufficient to point out that many evangelical leaders are not only misleading others with their teachings, but they are also living lives that are completely at odds with the modest lives lived by the men and the women we read about in the Bible. As one writer puts it: "The leading lights of today's Protestant faith in America are not merely inclined to endorse the notion that the rich are beloved by God—they are themselves rich, and cite their worldly success as evidence of God's favor."[35] In contrast, John the Baptist was imprisoned and later beheaded (Matt 14:1–12). Stephen was stoned to death (Acts 7:54–60). If God did not bless his most loyal servants in the Bible with what we would consider a blessed life here on earth, why should modern, typically Western, Christians believe he wants to bless

---

somewhere that tries to explain why some people might not be blessed financially. Usually the fault is laid at the feet of the tither who is only giving to get more (Alcorn, *Treasure Principle*, 72; Hood, *Take God at His Word*, 11–12). But when these same people teach that giving is the secret to receiving, are they not encouraging the very attitude of giving that they are simultaneously denouncing?

35. Lehmann, *Money Cult*, 13.

them with a wonderful life? Clearly something has gone wrong with the message of many evangelical churches.

Because tithing plays such a prominent role in church sermons, some may be surprised to discover that the earliest churches in America did not even teach tithing. In the early days of colonialism, churches were largely tax-funded.[36] Later, as churches were dropped from state-funding, churches raised money by renting pews.[37] However, this was controversial because it naturally led to the exclusion of the poor and gave the wealthy greater influence in the church. By the middle of the nineteenth century, pew-renting had mostly ceased and church funding became voluntary.[38] But voluntary giving led to another problem. How could churches get people to pay for something they could otherwise get for free? This remained a dilemma until about 1870, when a handful of influential writers began to argue that churches should be funded the same way that God funded the priests of ancient Israel.[39]

At first, tithing was a noble practice. The writers who promoted it were not encouraging people to tithe because it would benefit the giver, but because it would benefit the church. The link between tithing and prosperity would have to wait until another time in American history when Americans would become prosperous.

The beginning of the twentieth century brought difficult times for Americans, including two world wars and the Great Depression. However, after the Second World War, Americans began prospering like never before. Jobs were aplenty and a strong middle class was created. Families were moving from the cities into the suburbs and living lives that could only have been dreamed about during the Depression years.[40] The 1950s was also a time of religious fervor in America. "Never before in national history had as many Americans belonged to, attended, or associated themselves with religious institutions."[41] Americans were now both prosperous and religious and the time was ripe for false prophets to arise and associate the nascent prosperity with America's renewed interest in the Christian faith. It

---

36. Hudnut-Beumler, *Almighty's Dollar*, 9.
37. Hudnut-Beumler, *Almighty's Dollar*, 9–11.
38. Hudnut-Beumler, *Almighty's Dollar*, 12–13.
39. For a fuller discussion of this see: Hudnut-Beumler, *Almighty's Dollar*, 50–75.
40. See Hudnut-Beumler, *God in the Suburbs*, 2–8.
41. Hudnut-Beumler, *God in the Suburbs*, 1.

is no coincidence that it was during this period of time that tithing became linked with prosperity.

In the late 1940s and early 1950s a number of ministers broke away from Pentecostal churches to establish independent ministries. They were among the first to champion the idea that giving produces prosperity.[42] Oral Roberts declared that tithing was a "sure way for God to deliver you from poverty."[43] In 1954, he spoke of a "Blessing Pact" which would lead God to return any donation to the donor sevenfold.[44] His radio and television ministries would eventually expose even mainstream Christians to the prosperity gospel. Through the process of diffusion, the prosperity gospel made its way into churches of all denominations as Christian listeners and viewers took what sounded like a Christian message back into their local churches.[45] The prosperity gospel reached its apex in the 1980s and 1990s with the television ministries of Jim Bakker and Jimmy Swaggart, among others. Although both of their ministries ended in scandal,[46] the prosperity gospel that they preached penetrated into the homes of Christians spanning all evangelical denominations. Years later, one of these men would have a change of perspective on the prosperity gospel.

Jim Bakker, the disgraced former leader of the PTL, spent many years in prison, where he had time to reflect not only on his life, but also on his teachings. He no longer believes that giving leads to prosperity. In his book *I Was Wrong*, he writes: "For most of my life I believed that my understanding of God and how He wants us to live was not only correct but worth exporting to the world. One reason I have risked putting my heart into print is to tell you that my previous philosophy of life, out of which my attitudes and actions flowed, was fundamentally flawed. God does not promise that we will all be rich and prosperous, as I once preached. When

---

42. Harrell, *Oral Roberts*, 141.

43. Harrell, *All Things Are Possible*, 105.

44. Harrell, *Oral Roberts*, 141–42.

45. Harrell writes: "The success of the revival among the middle class not only put financial bonanzas within the reach of more moderate evangelists, it also pushed the charismatic message into the mainstream of American religion. Oral Roberts became a Methodist, and hundreds of clergymen in the traditional denominations . . . became filled with the Spirit. While some of these ministers established independent evangelistic associations, many remained within their denominations and tried to accommodate the charismatic experience to their own theological, liturgical, and ecclesiastical tradition" (*All Things Are Possible*, 227).

46. Vos, *Church History*, 166–67.

The Ninety-Sixth Thesis

I really studied the Bible while in prison, it became clear to me that not one man or woman—not even the prophets of God—led a life without pain."[47]

Five hundred years ago the Protestant Church was born out of Luther's grievances against the Catholic Church. It is a supreme irony of history that, five hundred years later, it is now a subset of the Protestant Church that is defrauding the faithful, namely evangelicals, with the misleading promise that God financially rewards those who tithe to their local church. The Catholic Church's teaching of indulgences and the evangelical movement's teaching of tithing-to-be-blessed are substantially the same and lead to the same result: in both cases, the church walks away with a bag of money and the Christian walks away with a bag full of empty promises.

I am losing faith in evangelical churches. What started out as a good movement with sincere intentions has become, over time, just another business in pursuit of the almighty dollar. This is not going unnoticed. How many times have we heard people say they do not want to go to church because the church only wants money?[48] Are they wrong?

There are some questions that remain. How should evangelical denominations and churches respond to this indictment? How should evangelicals respond to their churches in light of it? How should Christians give if tithing is not incumbent upon the church? What is the future of the evangelical movement? These questions will be addressed in the concluding chapter. For now, I want to move on and explain why, despite losing faith in the church, I found faith in Jesus Christ. The main reason for this is that I began finding answers to some of the most elusive questions about God. One of these questions concerned the obvious disconnect between the Bible and reality. The Bible records incredible stories about the miracles that Jesus and his disciples performed. However, these miracles do not seem to be happening today. The question is, why? The answer to this question is found in the close relationship between Jesus' miracles and his announcement of the arrival of the kingdom of God. It is to the subject of Jesus' miracles that I now turn.

---

47. Bakker, *I Was Wrong*, xiii.

48. Kelly writes about how the church's teaching of tithing has negatively impacted the reputation of the church. He writes, "the legalistic strict preaching of tithing has given many churches a bad reputation and a weak witness" (*Should the Church Teach Tithing?*, 166).

Chapter 2

Jesus' Miracles and the Kingdom of God

ONE OF THE MOST puzzling aspects of the modern church is the apparent lack of divine power, which manifests itself primarily through miracles. The Bible tells incredible stories about God's power, including how Jesus, among others, healed the sick and raised the dead. However, these miracles which play such a prominent role in the Bible are seemingly absent from the church today. The lack of such miracles has led to a lot of head scratching in the church. If God could perform miracles in biblical times, why is he not doing them today? Although there may be some denominations that would challenge the argument that miracles do not occur today, I think we can all agree that they are not occurring with either the same frequency or intensity as in New Testament times. The question is, why?

The topic of healings is a very confusing and controversial topic as is obvious from the fact that churches are all over the map on this subject. Some claim that miracles ceased with the closing of the apostolic age and thus should not be expected today.[1] Others claim that miraculous healings still occur. Neither position is without problems. A problem with the cessationist position is that it seems to derive more from perceived reality than from the Bible. Since miracles do not generally occur, cessationists assume that they never occur and then highlight those passages of scripture that appear to support their position while ignoring those that do not. A problem with the alternative position is that claims of the miraculous seem to occur only in denominations that promote the miraculous. Thus, it would

---

1. The term cessationist is used to describe those who take this position.

The Ninety-Sixth Thesis

seem that whether one believes that miracles happen has more to do with denominational affiliation than with anything else.

Pentecostal denominations are more likely to believe in and promote divine healing.[2] Such healings are usually performed by faith healers who are perhaps best-known from their roles as televangelists. The origins of today's faith healers can be traced back to at least the same charismatic tent-revivals of the late 1940s and early 1950s that produced the prosperity gospel.[3] Thus, there is a very close connection between the prosperity gospel and claims of miraculous healings with some of the same ministers promoting both.[4] Once again the name of Oral Roberts stands out.[5] Faith healers with Pentecostal backgrounds continue to claim that God works through them to bring healing to those in need. Many have attracted large followings, some of whom personally attest to God's healing power. Nevertheless, there are several reasons to be skeptical of many of these so-called miracles.

First, there have been, and continue to be, a lot of scams. Many faith healers have been proven to be false prophets who used their so-called "gift" for personal and financial gain.[6] In the 1980s, Peter Popoff amazed

---

2. Bowler writes: "Almost two-thirds of American pentecostals report that they have been healed or have seen another person healed, and it is clear that divine healing lays at the core of what captured prosperity believers' hearts" (*Blessed*, 140).

3. Harrell, *All Things Are Possible*, 5.

4. What started out primarily as a healing movement shifted over time toward a prosperity message. Harrell writes: "Perhaps the most important new idea of the charismatic revival was the emphasis on prosperity. The belief that God would grant prosperity to His people was an old tenet of the movement; even in the 1930s Thomas Wyatt had considered that doctrine the foundation of his ministry. But in the 1960s the message almost supplanted the earlier emphasis on healing; every evangelist came to advertise his own 'master key to financial success'" (*All Things Are Possible*, 229).

5. Harrell, *All Things Are Possible*, 49–50.

6. For those interested in this subject, I highly recommend James Randi's book *The Faith Healers*. This book completely exposes faith healers and their deceptive techniques. Audiences have been amazed when faith healers bring people in wheelchairs up on stage for healing and, moments later, they are walking! What the audience does not know is that these so-called "disabled" people were capable of walking before the healing! They were never disabled. Faith healers and their teams watch for people walking into their services with canes or walkers and then provide them with wheelchairs only to make it appear that they are disabled (Randi, *Faith Healers*, 105–7). Audiences have been similarly amazed when blind people are healed and able to tell the audience how many fingers the minister is holding up! What the audience does not know is that these so-called "blind" people could have told the faith healer how many fingers he was holding up before the healing! These individuals were not completely blind, but legally blind! These are just two of the deceptive techniques faith healers perform in the name of God to enrich

his audiences by being able to call out the names and ailments of people he had never met before and subsequently healing them.[7] However, he was eventually exposed as a fraud in 1986 on NBC's "Tonight Show" when James Randi, a magician and internationally known investigator of alleged paranormal abilities, informed Johnny Carson that he and his team discovered that Popoff's wife transferred that information to him via a wire transmitter from information that she and others had gathered from the audience upon entering the building![8] Thus, what appeared to be evidence of the miraculous turned out to be nothing but an elaborate scheme.

Second, there is a glaring disconnect between those who healed in the Bible and modern-day faith healers and that is that the latter are always asking for money. Where in the Bible did Jesus or any of his disciples ever ask for money when performing miracles? It never happened! Moreover, many faith healers have become fabulously wealthy and live lives that are completely at odds with the modest lives lived by the men and women we read about in the Bible.[9] Peter and John healed a crippled beggar at the temple and said something that very few of today's faith healers could say: "Silver and gold have we none!"[10]

Third, if miraculous healings do occur today, why is it that they never seem to make major headlines? It is inconceivable that in this day of advanced communication that so many people could be miraculously healed without attracting any attention from either the media or the medical community. In contrast, although Jesus healed at a time when there were no newspapers, radio, television or social media, the news of his healings spread like fire, even though he went out of his way to keep his miracles a secret.[11]

Fourth, when the media or medical community has investigated claims of miraculous healings, little evidence has been found to back up such claims. "In 1975, Dr. William A. Nolen, a noted Minnesota surgeon

---

themselves (Randi, Faith Healers, 104–5, 112–13).

7. Randi, Faith Healers, 142.

8. Randi, Faith Healers, 141–44, 150.

9. It is reported that Popoff's mail income alone was over one million dollars a month (Randi, Faith Healers, 68). Former Popoff controller Ira McCorriston told James Randi that the Popoffs' lavish lifestyle was being paid for with a number of five- and ten-dollar checks from older folks living on Social Security (Randi, Faith Healers, 69). Jim Bakker's PTL ministry is said to have been a $130-million-a-year operation (Randi, Faith Healers, 66).

10. Acts 3:6.

11. The significance of Jesus' emphasis on secrecy will be discussed in the chapter that follows.

The Ninety-Sixth Thesis

and author, included the case histories of twenty-six persons who believed they had been healed through the ministering of Kathryn Kuhlman in his book: *Healing: A Doctor in Search of a Miracle*. Dr. Nolen concluded that 'he couldn't find a single cured patient in the group.'"[12] But what about the claims of others who sincerely believed that they had been healed?[13] "*Life* magazine reported that the American Medical Association took the general position that all miracle cures were the result of either suggestion, spontaneous remission, or wrong diagnosis."[14] Even Oral Roberts admitted that it was possible that his healings were the result of psychosomatic illness.[15]

Fifth, many faith leaders insist that anyone can be healed provided that they have enough faith,[16] but strangely some of the leaders of the faith movement have died prematurely without healing.[17] Did they not have enough faith? If they were not healed, why should anyone accept their teaching that anyone can be healed provided that they have enough faith?

Sixth, I have attended church regularly for over twenty-five years and have yet to witness, or even meet anyone who has witnessed, a single miraculous healing. Although we have to be careful about evaluating what is or is not possible on the basis of our limited experience, the lack of miraculous healings in the church seems to be the rule not the exception. The blind always remain blind, the deaf always remain deaf, and the dead are never raised. The question is, why? Why would God perform such miracles in biblical times but not today?

---

12. Harrell, *All Things Are Possible*, 230. Nolen concluded his investigation with these words: "Two years ago I began looking for a healing miracle. When I started my search I hoped to find some evidence that someone, somewhere, had supernatural powers that he or she could employ to cure those patients we doctors, with all our knowledge and training, must still label 'incurable.' As I have said before, I have been unable to find any such miracle worker" (*Healing*, 272).

13. Faith healers often encourage those seeking divine healing to proclaim that healing and thank God for it as if it were already a foregone conclusion. Bowler writes: "Published guides for positive confession of healing and health ended with the prompt, 'Now praise Him for it!' as if it were already so" (*Blessed*, 143).

14. Harrell, *All Things Are Possible*, 101.

15. Nevertheless, Roberts insisted that his healings were still valuable (Harrell, *All Things Are Possible*, 156).

16. Some faith healers promote the power of faith to such a degree that they do not recommended taking medicine (see Harrell, *All Things Are Possible*, 86).

17. For example, faith healer A. A. Allen, who claimed to have healed so many, was unable to heal himself. He died at the age of fifty-nine from liver failure brought on by alcoholism (Randi, *Faith Healers*, 88).

Jesus' Miracles and the Kingdom of God

One reason for the confusion over miracles is that the Bible can be interpreted in different ways. But that does not mean that everyone's interpretation of the Bible is equally valid. With some exceptions, I would ignore much of what is taught in the church about this subject and turn to conservative biblical scholars for answers to difficult questions such as this.[18] One of the problems with the information that one may receive from any church is that the source of that information is not always well informed. Many churches allow anyone to become a church leader regardless of their level of theological education. Thus, the information that one may get about this and other subjects will not only vary from church to church, but also be limited by the leader's knowledge. In contrast, biblical scholars are usually well trained in a variety of subjects, including the Bible and biblical languages, and should not be as beholden to denominations and congregations that pay their salaries.[19] Thus, not only are they generally better informed,[20] but they can also be more authentic.

In order to understand why miracles, and in particular healings, are not occurring with either the same frequency or intensity as in New Testament times, we must understand why Jesus performed miracles in the first place. Some people think of Jesus as if he were some sort of wizard or magician who went from town to town in order to wow his audiences with magic. It is obvious that those who adhere to such a view are not well acquainted with the New Testament for, as we will see in the following chapter, Jesus went out of his way to keep his miracles a secret. However, there is a very specific reason why Jesus performed miracles and it is this reason that holds the clue as to why miracles should not be expected today. This reason is alluded to in a healing story recorded in Mark 2:1–12:

> A few days later, when Jesus again entered Capernaum, the people heard that he had come home. So many gathered that there was no room left, not even outside the door, and he preached the word to them. Some men came, bringing to him a paralytic, carried by four of them. Since they could not get him to Jesus because of the crowd, they made an opening in the roof above Jesus and, after digging through it, lowered the mat the paralyzed man was lying

---

18. I personally believe that there is more misinformation about God on Sunday than on any other day of the week.

19. Of course, there are exceptions to this too because some biblical scholars work for colleges that are denominationally affiliated.

20. There are some exceptions to this too. Some pastors are very well trained. It is only the ones who are not that concern me.

The Ninety-Sixth Thesis

on. When Jesus saw their faith, he said to the paralytic, "Son, your sins are forgiven." Now some teachers of the law were sitting there, thinking to themselves, "Why does this fellow talk like that? He's blaspheming! Who can forgive sins but God alone?" Immediately Jesus knew in his spirit that this was what they were thinking in their hearts, and he said to them, "Why are you thinking these things? Which is easier: to say to the paralytic, 'Your sins are forgiven,' or to say, 'Get up, take your mat and walk'? But that you may know that the Son of Man has authority on earth to forgive sins . . ." He said to the paralytic, "I tell you, get up, take your mat and go home." He got up, took his mat and walked out in full view of them all. This amazed everyone and they praised God, saying, "We have never seen anything like this!"

In this story four men brought a paralyzed man to Jesus for healing. When, however, the paralyzed man was lowered into the room, Jesus did not immediately heal him but rather told him that his sins have been forgiven. This was problematic for two reasons. First, this man did not come to have his sins forgiven, but to be able to walk again. Second, Jesus claimed that he had the power to forgive sins, something that only God could do. Naturally this angered those teachers of the law who were present. Knowing their thoughts, Jesus then asked them a question the significance of which is often misunderstood: "Is it easier to say to a paralytic 'get up and walk' or 'your sins are forgiven?'" Naturally it is easier to tell a paralytic that his sins have been forgiven than it is to tell him to get up and walk because anyone can tell someone that his sins have been forgiven and no one would ever know if that were true; claims about the metaphysical world (the world beyond) are unverifiable. However, if someone were to tell a paralytic to get up and walk, it would immediately be obvious whether or not that person had the power to heal. This was the situation that Jesus put himself in when he told the paralytic to stand up and walk. But—to the astonishment of everyone present that day—the paralytic stood up and walked! The point that must not be overlooked is how this healing gave credibility to Jesus' claim that he had the power to forgive sins. When the paralytic stood up and walked, Jesus' miracle demonstrated not only that he had the power to heal, but also that he had the power to forgive sins.

This story of the healing of the paralytic gives us insight into the real reason why Jesus performed miracles. Although Jesus had compassion for the paralytic and wanted to make him well, that was not the primary purpose of this healing. On the contrary, the primary purpose of it was to

Jesus' Miracles and the Kingdom of God

validate Jesus' claim that he had the power to forgive sins, a claim that would otherwise be beyond the realm of verification. How could those present know that Jesus really had the power to forgive sins? Because he had just done something that none of them had ever witnessed before; he had made a paralytic walk! Although this is just one of many healing stories in the New Testament, it holds the clue to understanding the primary purpose of Jesus' miracles and why they should not be expected today. Jesus performed miracles to validate his claims about the metaphysical world which would otherwise be beyond the realm of verification.

Jesus' claim that he had the power to forgive sins was part of a much broader and more significant claim that he made throughout the Gospels. When reading literature, it is important to pay attention to the first words spoken by important characters.[21] This applies to the Bible as well. The Gospel of Mark, the earliest of the four Gospels, records Jesus' first words as: "The time has come. . . . The kingdom of God is near. Repent and believe the good news!" (Mark 1:15). This announcement of the arrival of God's kingdom was the crux of Jesus' preaching as is obvious from the fact that everywhere he went he preached about it. Bright explains: "Everywhere the Kingdom of God is on his lips, and it is always a matter of desperate importance. What is it like? It is like a sower who goes forth to sow; it is like a costly pearl; it is like a mustard seed. How does one enter? One sells all that he has and gives to the poor; one becomes as a little child. Is it a matter of importance? Indeed it is! It would be better to mutilate yourself and enter maimed than not to get in at all."[22] The coming kingdom of God has been called the central theme of the Bible.[23] When Jesus announced that the kingdom of God had arrived, he was basically saying that it was time for everyone to get right with God because the long-anticipated kingdom of God which the Jews had been looking for since at least the destruction of Jerusalem at the hands of the Babylonians in 586 BC had finally arrived on earth. But what most people do not know about Jesus' announcement of the arrival of God's kingdom is that there is a very close relationship between it and the miracles that Jesus performed. Understanding this relationship is the key to understanding why miracles happened with so much frequency and intensity in New Testament times, but not so much today. However, before discussing this relationship

---

21. Alter, *Art of Biblical Narrative*, 74.
22. Bright, *Kingdom of God*, 17.
23. Bright suggests that if the Bible were given a title it could appropriately be called "The Book of the Coming Kingdom of God" (*Kingdom of God*, 197).

The Ninety-Sixth Thesis

and its significance it is necessary to give some background information on the kingdom of God that the Jews were anticipating.

Ancient Israel was a theocracy; God was Israel's king and Israel was his kingdom of priests who were chosen to teach the rest of the world about the one true God.[24] One of the earliest references to God as Israel's king occurs in one of the oldest poems of the Hebrew Bible, the Song of Moses. This poem says: "The LORD will *reign* for ever and ever" (Exod 15:18). Other allusions to God as Israel's king are found in the Old Testament book of Psalms.[25] Moreover, many Jewish prayers begin with the well-known phrase: "Blessed are you O Lord God *King* of the universe." The psalms and Jewish prayers do not say that God was king or that he will be king, but that he *is* king, even though at the present time he has chosen to keep his kingship veiled from humanity.

Because God is a king, he also has a kingdom. The notion of the kingdom of God is introduced in the Old Testament book of Exodus where Israel was chosen by God to be his people, called to live under his rule.[26] However, a few hundred years after the exodus from Egypt, the Israelites were no longer satisfied with a king who could not be seen with the human eye. Confronted with a formidable opponent in the Philistines, the Israelites wanted an earthly king to lead them into battle. This desire for an earthly king was not considered a complete and total rejection of the Lord as Israel's king. On the contrary, Israel viewed the earthly monarch as God's representative on earth.[27] Nevertheless, the Lord was not pleased with his people's request. Both the Lord and Samuel interpreted this request for a king as Israel's rejection of the Lord as her king. With the choice of Saul as Israel's first king, a new chapter was opened in the history of ancient Israel. The kingdom of God, which began with God's rule over his people at the time of the exodus, began to be viewed through the lens of a less than ideal monarchy.[28] Israel was still a theocracy, but that theocracy was now repre-

---

24. The Book of Exodus labels the Jewish people as a kingdom of priests (Exod 19:6). What do priests do? They teach others about God.

25. There are a number of psalms in the Old Testament that have been labeled royal psalms (Ps 2, 18, 20, 21, 45, 72, 93, 94, 95, 96, 97, 98, 99, 101, 110, 132, 144, et al.). These psalms concern the role of the king in the worship of the Lord. Many of them celebrate the Lord as Israel's king.

26. Bright, *Kingdom of God*, 28.

27. Storr writes: "The king ruled, not in his own right, but as selected by God, and as representing the people to God" (*From Abraham to Christ*, 260).

28. Bright writes: "Before Israel's hope of the Kingdom of God could assume such a

Jesus' Miracles and the Kingdom of God

sented for the most part by a corrupt and self-serving line of kings who, like all politicians, looked out primarily for their own interests.

After the time of King Solomon (930 BC), Israel split into two rival kingdoms, each with its own kings and priests. The kingdom of the north was called Israel and the kingdom of the south was called Judah. Eventually the kingdoms of Israel and Judah were destroyed, the former by the Assyrians in 722 BC and the latter by the Babylonians in 586 BC. The destruction of Judah and her capital, Jerusalem, by Nebuchadnezzar the king of Babylon in 586 BC closed the curtain on the kingdom of Judah as her last king was carried off into exile in Babylon. The rule of God over his people appeared to have come to an abrupt end.

During the period of the monarchy, however, prophets arose who spoke for God and warned of the coming destruction of these two kingdoms. These prophets were not blind to the shortcomings of the kings of Israel and Judah. They not only foretold the coming destruction of Israel and Judah at the hands of the Assyrians (722 BC) and Babylonians (586 BC), but also spoke of a time in the future when the kingdom of God would be restored. However, this coming kingdom of God would no longer be ruled by selfish individuals, such as the ones Israel and Judah had become accustomed to, but by a righteous ruler who would carry out God's will. This ruler would come to be known as the Messiah.[29] It is against this backdrop that we must understand Jesus' announcement of the arrival of God's kingdom.

The Jewish expectation was that at the end of history God would roll back the veil and make his reign manifest to all people by revealing the long-expected righteous ruler and descendant of king David who would come to take his throne. When Jesus announced the arrival of God's kingdom, he was basically saying that the long-expected kingdom that the Jews had been waiting for had finally arrived on earth and that he was the anticipated ruler, the Messiah, whom the prophets had foretold would one day come to take the Davidic throne.

According to the NIV, Jesus announced that "the kingdom of God is near" (Mark 1:14–15). However, the NIV does not completely capture the perfect tense of the Greek verbs. A literal translation of Jesus' announcement is: "The time *has been fulfilled* and the kingdom of God *has come*

---

form, she had first to build a kingdom on this earth" (*Kingdom of God*, 19).

29. Ludwig writes: "It is from the role of the king as the deliverer of Israel that the notion of the 'messiah' arose in Israel. Originally the term messiah, which means 'anointed one,' applied to the king as the one anointed to lead Yahweh's people" (*Sacred Paths of the West*, 101).

The Ninety-Sixth Thesis

near."³⁰ Jesus was saying that the long-expected kingdom of God was now a present reality. This is affirmed by Luke, who writes:

> Jesus was driving out a demon that was mute. When the demon left, the man who had been mute spoke, and the crowd was amazed. But some of them said, "By Beelzebub, the prince of demons, he is driving out demons." Others tested him by asking for a sign from heaven. Jesus knew their thoughts and said to them: "Any kingdom divided against itself will be ruined, and a house divided against itself will fall. If Satan is divided against himself, how can his kingdom stand? I say this because you claim that I drive out demons by Beelzebub. Now if I drive out demons by Beelzebub, by whom do your followers drive them out? So then, they will be your judges. But if I drive out demons by the finger of God, *then the kingdom of God has come to you.*" (Luke 11:14–20)

Now if the kingdom of God really had arrived on earth in the days of Jesus, we would naturally expect the world to be a different place than it was before its arrival. It is against this backdrop that we must understand Jesus' miracles.

As already noted, there is a very close relationship between Jesus' announcement of the arrival of God's kingdom and the miracles that he performed.³¹ This relationship is clearly seen from the fact that they are frequently mentioned together in the same passages. In Matt 10:5–8 Jesus gave his twelve disciples the following instructions:

> These twelve Jesus sent out with the following instructions: "Do not go among the Gentiles or enter any town of the Samaritans. Go rather to the lost sheep of Israel. *As you go, preach this message: 'The kingdom of heaven is near.' Heal the sick, raise the dead, cleanse those who have leprosy, drive out demons.*"

In this passage, Jesus told his disciples to do two things: first, announce the arrival of God's kingdom and, second, perform miracles. That the announcement and the miracles are closely related to each other is confirmed by other passages where the two occur in tandem.

---

30. Author's translation.

31. Matthew refers to the kingdom of God as the "kingdom of heaven," while Luke refers to it as the "kingdom of God." The terms are synonymous. The difference is that Matthew is writing for a Jewish audience, who do not pronounce the name of God for fear of violating the commandment not to take the name of the Lord in vain (Exod 20:7), while Luke is writing for a Gentile audience, who have no scruples about using the divine name.

Jesus' Miracles and the Kingdom of God

Jesus went throughout Galilee, teaching in their synagogues, *preaching the good news of the kingdom, and healing every disease and sickness* among the people. (Matt 4:23)

When the apostles returned, they reported to Jesus what they had done. Then he took them with him and they withdrew by themselves to a town called Bethsaida, but the crowds learned about it and followed him. *He welcomed them and spoke to them about the kingdom of God, and healed those who needed healing.* (Luke 9:10–11)

After this the Lord appointed seventy-two others and sent them two by two ahead of him to every town and place where he was about to go. He told them, "The harvest is plentiful, but the workers are few. Ask the Lord of the harvest, therefore, to send out workers into his harvest field. Go! I am sending you out like lambs among wolves.... When you enter a town and are welcomed, eat what is set before you. *Heal the sick who are there and tell them, 'The kingdom of God is near you.'"* (Luke 10:1–3, 8–9)

It is obvious from these passages that the announcement of the arrival of God's kingdom and the miracles are related to one another, but in what way? The clue comes from the story of Jesus' healing of the paralytic.

In the story of Jesus' healing of the paralytic, we learned that the healing was done not merely to make the paralytic well again, but even more so to validate Jesus' claim that he had the power to forgive sins. The miracle was thus a sign that Jesus did indeed have the power to forgive sins.[32] In a similar way, Jesus performed all his miracles to authenticate his broader claim that the kingdom of God had arrived on earth. How would people know that the kingdom of God really had arrived on earth and that the world was now a different place? Because of the miracles that Jesus and his disciples were performing. Jesus' miracles were signs of the dawning of a new age; signs that the kingdom of God had broken into the world and that the world was now a different place. This conclusion finds confirmation from the story of John the Baptist.

John the Baptist is best known for having baptized Jesus in the Jordan river (Matt 3:13–17) and for having inaugurated Jesus' earthly ministry. He was also related to Jesus (Luke 1:36). When baptizing Jesus, John witnessed the Holy Spirit's miraculous descent on Jesus in the form of a dove (John

---

32. Interestingly, John's gospel uses the Greek word "signs" for Jesus' miracles.

1:32). At this early point in John's ministry, he was extremely confident that Jesus was the long-anticipated Jewish Messiah. John's testimony regarding Jesus is recorded in the Gospel of John 1:29–34:

> The next day John saw Jesus coming toward him and said, "Look, the Lamb of God, who takes away the sin of the world! This is the one I meant when I said, 'A man who comes after me has surpassed me because he was before me.' I myself did not know him, but the reason I came baptizing with water was that he might be revealed to Israel." Then John gave this testimony: "I saw the Spirit come down from heaven as a dove and remain on him. I would not have known him, except that the one who sent me to baptize with water told me, 'The man on whom you see the Spirit come down and remain is he who will baptize with the Holy Spirit.' I have seen and I testify that this is the Son of God."

However, there is one potentially embarrassing detail of John's life that is rarely, if ever, mentioned in church. Sometime after John baptized Jesus, John began to entertain doubts about whether Jesus was the Messiah.[33] Matthew 11:2–3 reads: "When John heard in prison what Christ was doing, he sent his disciples to ask him, 'Are you the one who was to come, or should we expect someone else?'" What caused John to begin having doubts about Jesus and how does this relate to our discussion of miracles and the kingdom of God?

As we know from both the Gospels of Matthew and Luke, John the Baptist had been imprisoned by Herod (a son of Herod the Great) because John had confronted Herod regarding his unlawful relationship with his brother Phillip's wife (Matt 14:1–12; Luke 3:19–20). Prison, so it must have seemed to John, did not seem to square well with Jesus' announcement that the kingdom of God had finally arrived on earth and that a new age had dawned. If God's kingdom really had arrived, as Jesus had preached, then the world should be a different place where good triumphs over evil. However, John's imprisonment seemed to contradict that. Thus, John sent his disciples to ask Jesus if he really was the one who was to come, or whether another ruler should be expected (Matt 11:2–3).

Jesus' response to John's question is very insightful. "Jesus replied, 'Go back and report to John what you hear and see: The blind receive sight, the

---

33. One of the things I appreciate about the Bible is its honesty. The writers could have easily left this piece of information out, but they did not. John's wrestling with his faith should be comforting to all of us, for who among us has not entertained doubts from time to time?

Jesus' Miracles and the Kingdom of God

lame walk, those who have leprosy are cured, the deaf hear, the dead are raised, and the good news is preached to the poor. Blessed is the man who does not fall away on account of me'" (Matt 11:4–6). In short, Jesus was saying: "The world *is* different now, John! God's kingdom has arrived and the evidence of that is the miracles that I am performing."

But here is where things become complicated. Jesus spoke of the kingdom of God in two different tenses. On the one hand, Jesus announced that the kingdom of God had arrived and was a present reality (Luke 11:20), but, on the other hand, he spoke as if that kingdom were yet to come. An example of this is in the Lord's prayer where Jesus taught his disciples to pray for the kingdom to come (Matt 6:10). Why was Jesus teaching his disciples to pray for the kingdom to come if it were already a present reality? Moreover, to what extent had the kingdom of God arrived in the days of Jesus? Very few people, apart from Jesus' disciples, seem to have been aware of it. The Romans and Jews certainly did not recognize the arrival of another kingdom; business and daily life went on as usual for the vast majority of people. Good did not appear to be triumphing over evil either, as was obvious from the fact that a righteous man like John could be unjustly imprisoned. But this leaves a perplexing problem. Had God's kingdom really arrived on earth, as Jesus taught, or was it yet to come, as Jesus also taught?

In order to answer this question, it is imperative that we understand that the kingdom of God is inextricably tied to the person of Jesus. When Jesus was here two thousand years ago, God's kingdom was here because Jesus the king was here.[34] The kingdom, at that time, could indeed be described as a present reality and the miracles that Jesus performed were evidence of that reality. However, it is also important to note that Jesus' kingdom was here only in a veiled sense. Jesus did not arrive with all the pomp of an earthly monarch and overwhelm his enemies. For the vast majority of people, business and daily life went on as usual. For some reason, Jesus wanted to keep his kingdom somewhat of a secret; he did not want either the political structures of his day or the rank-and-file masses to discover who he was; only his disciples and select others were permitted to know his true identity. This "Messianic Secret" is the subject of the next chapter. All these details are important pieces of a puzzle that will come together only when all the evidence from later chapters is included. For now, it is important to observe

---

34. Bright writes: "What all the ages have desired to see now is here—in this Jesus" (*Kingdom of God*, 197). Later he adds: "In the person and work of Jesus the Kingdom of God has intruded into the world" (*Kingdom of God*, 216).

The Ninety-Sixth Thesis

that while Jesus could legitimately say that the kingdom of God was a present reality when he was here two thousand years ago, it was here only in a veiled sense because he chose not to make it obvious to everyone. Moreover, this kingdom of God which Jesus had spoken of as a present reality was here only temporarily because Jesus the king would die on the cross for the sins of the world and subsequently return to his father. At that point, the kingdom of God was no longer a present reality; it was now yet to come. It could no longer be said that the kingdom of God had arrived, but that the kingdom of God will arrive. Thus, we pray "thy kingdom come."[35]

The failure to understand this distinction has led to a lot of confusion and false teachings in the church. Jesus and his disciples performed miracles as a way to authenticate the arrival of God's kingdom. The miracles that Jesus and his disciples performed were signs of the kingdom; signs that God's power had broken into the world and that a new age had dawned. But this new age did not last long because Jesus had to complete his mission by dying on the cross for the sins of the world. When that happened, the kingdom of God—and all the miracles associated with it—were no longer a present reality, but suddenly became yet to come. The kingdom of God which Jesus proclaimed as a present reality was merely a foretaste of the kingdom of God that will come in full manifestation at the end of history. Thus, we should not expect to see the kinds of miracles that we read about in the New Testament—the signs of the kingdom—until the king and his kingdom return to earth. At that time, those miracles which were limited in scope (both geographically and in extent) in the days of Jesus will be manifest in a way unheard of even in New Testament times. Not just some of the sick will be healed, but all the sick will be healed. Moreover, healings will not be limited to the borders of ancient Israel, but will be manifest throughout the entire world. Most importantly, it will be a kingdom without end. That is the kingdom of God for which all humanity and nature eagerly awaits.

Does this mean that miracles are not possible today? Absolutely not! It would be a mistake to categorically state that miracles never happen. The world is far too large and complex to make a generalization such as that. Miracles occasionally happened in Old Testament times—before Jesus came—and they may even occasionally happen today. God is God and can intervene in the affairs of the world anytime he chooses. All that is being

---

35. Scholars have long recognized this tension in Jesus' teaching of the kingdom of God and refer to it with the phrase "now and not yet." The kingdom of God was a present reality in the days of Jesus (thus, now), but it was also yet to come (thus, not yet).

Jesus' Miracles and the Kingdom of God

argued in this chapter is that miracles should not be expected with the same frequency or intensity as in the days of Jesus because the kingdom of God is no longer a present reality, but is now yet to come. Thus, it is not entirely accurate to say that miracles have ceased and are no longer possible. Rather, it is more accurate to say that Jesus the king, the one who had the authority to perform miracles and to give that authority to others, is no longer on earth. Jesus and his kingdom are now yet to come.

Some may legitimately ask, if miracles were signs of the kingdom, why then were the disciples able to perform miracles even after Jesus' ascension into heaven? As we have learned, Jesus had given the twelve (Matt 10:1), as well as at least seventy others (Luke 10:1–20), the authority to perform miracles. They were given this authority for one reason and that was to validate the claim that God's kingdom had arrived on earth. This is clear from those passages highlighted above where the miracles and the announcement of the arrival of God's kingdom occur in tandem. We do not have to assume that this authority was abruptly taken away from the disciples the moment that Jesus ascended into heaven. They still possessed this authority to perform miracles.[36] However, there were clearly limitations to the authority that had been granted to them; unlike Jesus, they were not always able to perform miracles.[37] The mistake that modern faith healers make is that they naively assume that this same authority is available to them or anyone else

---

36. In 1 Cor 12:28 Paul writes about those who in his day had the gift of healing. The disciples were still alive when Paul wrote his letters to the various churches. This is clear from the fact that Paul met some of them, including Peter, James, and John (Gal 1:18–19; 2:1–14). When Paul writes about this gift, was he referring to the authority that had been granted to the disciples by Jesus? This is very likely; however, this is a complicated issue that is outside the scope of this book and that requires a book itself. What is clear is that most, if not all, of those who claim to possess this gift today, do not. There is little to no evidence to back up such claims, but a lot of evidence of outright fraud.

37. When reading the New Testament, it is easy to get the impression that the disciples could heal at will, like Jesus could. However, a careful reading of it reveals otherwise. An example of this is Matt 17:14–16: When they came to the crowd, a man approached Jesus and knelt before him. "Lord, have mercy on my son," he said. "He has seizures and is suffering greatly. He often falls into the fire or into the water. I brought him to your disciples, but they could not heal him." Paul healed people at times (Acts 20:7–12; Acts 28:8), but on other occasions seems to have been unable to do so. In Phil 2:25–30, Paul writes about the deep concern he had for his companion Epaphroditus who was sick and near death. If Paul could heal at will, there would have been no reason for him to be concerned about his friend's health. Sometimes when reading the Bible, it is just as important to read between the lines as it is to read the words themselves.

who simply reads these passages. They have failed to differentiate between what has been called the descriptive and the prescriptive.

There are two kinds of passages in the Bible. Some passages are *descriptive* and thus *describe* events that happened in the past. Much of the Old Testament is descriptive. An example is Gen 12:10–20:

> Now there was a famine in the land, and Abram went down to Egypt to live there for a while because the famine was severe. As he was about to enter Egypt, he said to his wife Sarai, "I know what a beautiful woman you are. When the Egyptians see you, they will say, 'This is his wife.' Then they will kill me but will let you live. Say you are my sister, so that I will be treated well for your sake and my life will be spared because of you." When Abram came to Egypt, the Egyptians saw that she was a very beautiful woman. And when Pharaoh's officials saw her, they praised her to Pharaoh, and she was taken into his palace. He treated Abram well for her sake, and Abram acquired sheep and cattle, male and female donkeys, menservants and maidservants, and camels. But the LORD inflicted serious diseases on Pharaoh and his household because of Abram's wife Sarai. So Pharaoh summoned Abram. "What have you done to me?" he said. "Why didn't you tell me she was your wife? Why did you say, 'She is my sister,' so that I took her to be my wife? Now then, here is your wife. Take her and go!" Then Pharaoh gave orders about Abram to his men, and they sent him on his way, with his wife and everything he had.

These verses have no personal application for readers today; they merely *describe* an event that happened in the past.[38] Descriptive passages such as this are still important for the reader in the sense that they teach who God is and how he worked in the past to bring about salvation, but they are not personally applicable to the reader.

Descriptive passages are not limited to the Old Testament but are also found in the New Testament. An example is 2 Tim 4:9–13, where Paul gives Timothy personal instructions.

> Do your best to come to me quickly, for Demas, because he loved this world, has deserted me and has gone to Thessalonica. Crescens has gone to Galatia, and Titus to Dalmatia. Only Luke is with me. Get Mark and bring him with you, because he is helpful to me

---

38. There is a tendency in the church to extract some kind of life lesson from every passage or to force an interpretation upon the text that is really not there. However, as Gen 12:10–20 illustrates, not every biblical passage contains personal application for the reader. Many passages simply give information about events that happened in the past.

Jesus' Miracles and the Kingdom of God

in my ministry. I sent Tychicus to Ephesus. When you come, bring the cloak that I left with Carpus at Troas, and my scrolls, especially the parchments.

Clearly these instructions are for a companion of Paul named Timothy who lived two thousand years ago and do not contain any personal application for the modern reader.

Prescriptive verses, on the other hand, *prescribe* how Christians should live today and usually contain injunctions or commands that are timeless and thus apply equally to the ancient and modern reader. An example is Jesus' command to love God and neighbor. Clearly loving God and neighbor is a timeless command that applies equally to every one of every age. The mistake that many Christians—especially faith healers—make today is that they fail to distinguish between passages that are descriptive and prescriptive and read every passage as if it speaks directly and personally to them. Matthew 10:1 can be used as a good illustration.

Matthew 10:1 reads: "Jesus called his twelve disciples to him and gave *them* authority to drive out evil spirits and to heal every disease and sickness." A descriptive reading of this verse understands it as describing an event that happened in the past between Jesus and his disciples. It is thus informative and contains no personal application for the reader. A prescriptive reading of this passage understands it as having personal application for the modern reader such as when faith healers read it and assume that the healing power Jesus gave to his disciples is also available to them. But this is clearly a misinterpretation of this verse. First, it *describes* an event that happened in the past between a very specific group of people, Jesus and his twelve disciples. Second, the verse clearly states that Jesus gave this authority to *them* (the twelve). There is no indication anywhere in this passage that this power is available to the reader. Third, the disciples were given this authority for a specific reason: to authenticate the arrival of the kingdom of God. This is clear from vv. 7–8, which read: "As you go, preach this message: 'The kingdom of heaven is near. Heal the sick, raise the dead, cleanse those who have leprosy, drive out demons.'" If this same power were available to the reader, there would be no reason to pray for the kingdom to come because the signs of the kingdom (the miracles) would not be something yet to come, but could be manifest anywhere, at any time, during any age. Fourth, there are no commands or injunctions in this verse that would suggest any personal application for the reader. Finally, the most obvious problem with a prescriptive interpretation of this verse is that, when faith healers attempt to perform these miracles, there is very limited evidence of success and a lot of evidence of outright fraud.[39]

Of course, modern-day faith healers will point to other scriptures to back up their claims. One of their favorite verses is Matt 17:20, in which Jesus says: "If you have faith as small as a mustard seed, you can say to this mountain, 'Move from here to there,' and it will move. Nothing will be impossible for you." However, this passage only reinforces why it is so important to have a proper understanding of the difference between the descriptive and the prescriptive. In this passage, and in so many others like it, Jesus was speaking to his disciples to whom he had given this authority, not to us who simply read these passages.

The conclusion of this chapter is that Jesus performed miracles to validate his claim that the long-anticipated kingdom of God had finally arrived on earth. How would people know that the kingdom of God had finally arrived on earth? Because of the miracles that Jesus and his disciples were performing. But there is something strange about this conclusion and that is that there are a number of passages in the New Testament where Jesus goes out of his way to keep his miracles a secret. Why would Jesus perform miracles to validate his claim that God's kingdom had finally arrived on earth, but then prevent the vast majority of people from witnessing or even hearing about his miracles? The answer to this question holds the clue to unlocking many of the mysteries of God. It is to the subject of secrecy in Jesus' ministry that we now turn.

---

39. I personally think that evangelicals must find a way to distance themselves from faith healers. I am not suggesting that Christians should not pray for healing. They should! The Bible encourages this. What I am saying is that we must be very skeptical about the claims of those who say they have this gift. The Epistle of James does not seem to be aware of people who possessed the gift of healing. It encourages the elders of the church to anoint the sick and pray (Jas 5:14–15). This is one of the clearest indications that there never was a class of people who possessed the gift of healing and that when Paul referred to this gift (1 Cor 12:9), he was referring to the disciples who received it directly from the Lord.

Chapter 3

The Messianic Secret

ONE ASPECT OF JESUS' teaching that is not widely known is his emphasis on secrecy. Jesus criticized the Pharisees, the religious leaders of his day, for going out of their way to show people how religious they were (Matt 23:5–7). They sounded trumpets when they gave to the poor (Matt 6:1–2). They prayed in public places to be seen by men (Matt 6:5–8). They disfigured their faces so that it would be obvious that they were fasting (Matt 6:16). Jesus taught his disciples not to be like such people. Although on the outside they appear to be sincere, their hearts tell a different story (Matt 23:25–28). In contrast, Jesus taught that the faith should be practiced in total secrecy. When we give, we are to give with such secrecy that our left hand should not know what our right hand is giving (Matt 6:1–4). When we pray, we are to pray in a secret room where no one can see us (Matt 6:5–8).[1] When we fast, we are to do everything we can to prevent others from knowing that we are fasting (Matt 6:16–18). But what is surprising and completely unknown to most Christians is that Jesus went out of his way to keep his miracles a secret. The question is, why?

Luke 9:28–36 records the following story:

> About eight days after Jesus said this, he took Peter, John and James with him and went up onto a mountain to pray. As he was praying, the appearance of his face changed, and his clothes became as bright as a flash of lightning. Two men, Moses and Elijah, appeared in glorious splendor, talking with Jesus. They spoke about

---

1. It should be no surprise then that Jesus often went to a solitary place to pray (Matt 14:23; Luke 6:12).

The Ninety-Sixth Thesis

his departure, which he was about to bring to fulfillment at Jerusalem. Peter and his companions were very sleepy, but when they became fully awake, they saw his glory and the two men standing with him. As the men were leaving Jesus, Peter said to him, "Master, it is good for us to be here. Let us put up three shelters one for you, one for Moses and one for Elijah." (He did not know what he was saying.) While he was speaking, a cloud appeared and enveloped them, and they were afraid as they entered the cloud. A voice came from the cloud, saying, "This is my Son, whom I have chosen; listen to him." When the voice had spoken, they found that Jesus was alone. The disciples kept this to themselves, and told no one at that time what they had seen.

This story, called the Transfiguration of Jesus, is remarkable for several obvious reasons. First, Peter, James, and John were granted the unique privilege of seeing Jesus as he would have appeared in the world-beyond. Second, they saw Moses and Elijah standing before them talking to Jesus. This won't seem like a big deal unless the reader has some understanding of biblical chronology. Moses and Elijah had been dead for hundreds of years by the time of the transfiguration![2] And third, these three disciples heard the voice of God speak from heaven. What a day! It is not hard to imagine each of them bursting with excitement to get back down the mountain to tell everyone what they had seen and heard. But perhaps the most remarkable detail of this story is the one that comes last. According to the Gospel of Luke, these three disciples kept these things to themselves and did not tell anyone what they had seen or heard that day. The question is, why? How could anyone possibly keep such astonishing events a secret? The Gospel of Luke does not answer this question. Fortunately, there are two other Gospel accounts of this story that fill in the missing detail.

The story of the transfiguration of Jesus is recorded not only in the Gospel of Luke, but also in the Gospels of Matthew and Mark. Their accounts give additional information that explains the disciples' silence regarding what happened that day. According to their accounts, the disciples did not tell anyone what they had seen or heard because Jesus had given them strict orders not to tell anyone.

---

2. Moses lived at least twelve hundred years before Jesus, while Elijah lived approximately seven hundred years before Jesus.

The Messianic Secret

> As they were coming down the mountain, Jesus gave them orders not to tell anyone what they had seen until the Son of Man had risen from the dead. (Mark 9:9)[3]

> As they were coming down the mountain, Jesus instructed them, "Don't tell anyone what you have seen, until the Son of Man has been raised from the dead." (Matt 17:9)

The observation that Jesus wanted the disciples to keep the details of his transfiguration a secret until he had risen from the dead is puzzling and requires further investigation. It is not hard to imagine the disciples reasoning among themselves about all the good that could result from widespread knowledge of what transpired that day. But those who regularly read the New Testament know that this was not the only time that Jesus requested that his disciples keep silent about something they had witnessed. There are a number of passages in the Gospels where Jesus performed miracles, but then warned those present not to tell anyone what they had seen or heard.[4]

> A man with leprosy came to him and begged him on his knees, "If you are willing, you can make me clean." Filled with compassion, Jesus reached out his hand and touched the man. "I am willing," he said. "Be clean!" Immediately the leprosy left him and he was cured. Jesus sent him away at once with a strong warning: "*See that you don't tell this to anyone. But go, show yourself to the priest and offer the sacrifices that Moses commanded for your cleansing, as a testimony to them.*" (Mark 1:40–44)

> After he put them all out, he took the [dead] child's father and mother and the disciples who were with him, and went in where the child was. He took her by the hand and said to her, "Talitha koum!" (which means, "Little girl, I say to you, get up!"). Immediately the girl stood up and walked around (she was twelve years old). At this they were completely astonished. *He gave strict orders not to let anyone know about this,* and told them to give her something to eat. (Mark 5:40–43)

---

3. The phrase "Son of Man" is a title that Jesus often used in reference to himself. It is noteworthy that Jesus never calls himself the Messiah, but rather refers to himself with this cryptic phrase. Many books have been written on this topic. For two good, but brief, discussions of this term and its significance, see Wright, *Knowing Jesus*, 148–53; Carroll, *Christ Actually*, 97–103.

4. Although Jesus' emphasis on secrecy is most prominent in the Synoptic Gospels (Matthew, Mark, and Luke), there are allusions to it in the Gospel of John as well (see John 7:1–4; 10:22–24).

The Ninety-Sixth Thesis

> Then Jesus left the vicinity of Tyre and went through Sidon, down to the Sea of Galilee and into the region of the Decapolis. There some people brought to him a man who was deaf and could hardly talk, and they begged him to place his hand on the man. After he took him aside, away from the crowd, Jesus put his fingers into the man's ears. Then he spit and touched the man's tongue. He looked up to heaven and with a deep sigh said to him, "Ephphatha!" (which means, "Be opened!"). At this, the man's ears were opened, his tongue was loosened and he began to speak plainly. *Jesus commanded them not to tell anyone.* But the more he did so, the more they kept talking about it. (Mark 7:31–36)

> They came to Bethsaida, and some people brought a blind man and begged Jesus to touch him. He took the blind man by the hand and led him outside the village. When he had spit on the man's eyes and put his hands on him, Jesus asked, "Do you see anything?" He looked up and said, "I see people; they look like trees walking around." Once more Jesus put his hands on the man's eyes. Then his eyes were opened, his sight was restored, and he saw everything clearly. Jesus sent him home, saying, *"Don't go into the village."* (Mark 8:22–26)

For some reason, Jesus wanted to keep both his transfiguration and his miracles a secret. The question is, why? The only clue comes from the account of the transfiguration where Jesus told the disciples not to tell anyone what they had seen or heard *until Jesus had risen from the dead* (Matt 17:9 and Mark 9:9). Why is this detail so important?

A careful reading of the New Testament reveals that Jesus kept other secrets. For example, Jesus drove out demons and then forbade them from speaking because they knew who he was.

> They went to Capernaum, and when the Sabbath came, Jesus went into the synagogue and began to teach. The people were amazed at his teaching, because he taught them as one who had authority, not as the teachers of the law. Just then a man in their synagogue who was possessed by an evil spirit cried out, "What do you want with us, Jesus of Nazareth? Have you come to destroy us? I know who you are—the Holy One of God!" *"Be quiet!"* said Jesus sternly. "Come out of him!" (Mark 1:21–25)

> That evening after sunset the people brought to Jesus all the sick and demon-possessed. The whole town gathered at the door, and Jesus healed many who had various diseases. He also drove out

The Messianic Secret

many demons, *but he would not let the demons speak because they knew who he was.* (Mark 1:32–34)

Whenever the evil spirits saw him, they fell down before him and cried out, "You are the Son of God." *But he gave them strict orders not to tell who he was.* (Mark 3:11–12)

If we put all these clues from all these passages together it would seem that Jesus did not want the masses to discover that he was the Messiah. But if that conclusion were not entirely clear from the passages above, that is the inescapable conclusion of Mark 8:27–30.

Jesus and his disciples went on to the villages around Caesarea Philippi. On the way he asked them, "Who do people say I am?" They replied, "Some say John the Baptist; others say Elijah; and still others, one of the prophets." "But what about you?" he asked. "Who do you say I am?" Peter answered, "You are the Christ." *Jesus warned them not to tell anyone about him.*

The conclusion that Jesus did not want those outside of his inner circle of disciples to know that he was the Messiah is one of the details of Jesus' life that even most Christians have never heard, as this detail is conveniently left out of church sermons. There are likely two reasons for this. First, it is not easy to understand why Jesus wanted to keep his identity as the Messiah a secret. Thus, many choose to ignore difficult passages such as these rather than try to understand them. Second, Jesus' desire to conceal his identity in these passages is inconsistent with other passages in the New Testament that teach that Jesus came that people might believe in him. For example, in the Great Commission, Jesus told his disciples to make disciples of all nations by baptizing them in the name of the Father, the Son, and the Holy Spirit (Matt 28:19). But how could they make disciples of all nations in the name of the Father, Son, and Holy Spirit if they were not permitted to reveal Jesus as the Messiah?

The clue to solving this conundrum is found in the story of the transfiguration. "As they were coming down the mountain, Jesus gave them orders not to tell anyone what they had seen *until the Son of Man had risen from the dead*" (Mark 9:9). Why is this detail so important? Why was it necessary that the disciples not tell anyone about Jesus' miracles or identity until after his resurrection? The answer must be that widespread knowledge of Jesus' miracles would have betrayed his identity as the Messiah and would have somehow prevented him from dying on the cross and subsequently

The Ninety-Sixth Thesis

rising from the dead. The question is, how would widespread knowledge of Jesus' identity as the Messiah have prevented him from rising from the dead? And why would this be a problem? Did Jesus want to die?

Traditionally Christians have blamed both the Jews and the Romans for the death of Jesus. The reality is that only Jesus is to blame. Had Jesus been forthright about his identity as the Messiah and allowed everyone to witness his miracles, the Jews would have gladly welcomed him as the Messiah and would have begged him to immediately set up his kingdom.[5] On at least one occasion, this almost happened. After having witnessed the miracle of the feeding of the five thousand, the crowds tried to "make him king by force" (John 6:1–15). But Jesus could not allow this to happen and thus slipped away (John 6:15). The reason for this is very insightful. Jesus came to earth with a very specific plan and that plan was to die on the cross for the sins of the world. That was Jesus' mission and absolutely nothing could be allowed to prevent that from happening. Widespread knowledge of Jesus' miracles would have derailed Jesus' plan because his miracles would have betrayed his identity, the very thing that he was trying to protect. The rank-and-file masses would never have allowed a miracle-working Messiah to die on the cross for the sins of the world. Thus, Jesus had to keep his miracles and his identity as the Messiah a secret until after he had accomplished his plan, namely until after he had risen from the dead (Matt 17:9 and Mark 9:9).

The conclusion that Jesus' plan required that he keep both his miracles and his identity a secret until after he had risen from the dead is supported by a full reading of Mark 8:27–30, the passage highlighted above in which Jesus warned his disciples not to tell anyone that he was the Messiah. When Jesus asked the disciples who people thought he was, the disciples responded by saying, "Some say John the Baptist; others say Elijah; and still others, one of the prophets" (Mark 8:28). Then he asked them all point blank, "Who do you all think I am?" Peter responded: "You are the Christ" (Mark 8:29).[6] Jesus then warned them not to tell anyone about this (Mark 8:30). Unfortunately, some modern Bibles, such as the NIV, insert an artificial break at this point and separate vv. 30 and 31, however, these verses should be read together as originally intended.[7] In v. 30 Jesus warned the disciples

---

5. A miracle-working Messiah was, of course, more in line with their expectations.

6. The title "Christ" is the Greek equivalent of the Hebrew "Messiah."

7. These "breaks" with headings, like verses in general, are a modern convention; they are not found in ancient manuscripts. In ancient texts, everything ran together.

not to tell anyone that he is the Messiah and v. 31 explains why. "He then began to teach them that the Son of Man *must* suffer many things and be rejected by the elders, chief priests and teachers of the law, and that he *must* be killed and after three days rise again" (Mark 8:30–31). That this is not some random arrangement is indicated by Matthew and Luke's accounts of this same story, both of which also place Jesus' prediction of his death immediately after his warning to his disciples (Matt 16:13–21; Luke 9:18–22). The NIV does not insert an artificial break in Luke's account of this story, which makes it easier to discern the relationship between Jesus' warning and his prediction of his death. It reads:

> Once when Jesus was praying in private and his disciples were with him, he asked them, "Who do the crowds say I am?" They replied, "Some say John the Baptist; others say Elijah; and still others, that one of the prophets of long ago has come back to life." "But what about you?" he asked. "Who do you say I am?" Peter answered, "The Christ of God." Jesus strictly warned them not to tell this to anyone. And he said, "The Son of Man must suffer many things and be rejected by the elders, chief priests and teachers of the law, and he must be killed and on the third day be raised to life."

Why must the disciples not tell anyone that Jesus is the Messiah? Because Jesus must be killed and subsequently raised back to life. That was Jesus' mission and absolutely nothing could be allowed to interfere with it.

The picture of Jesus that emerges from this study is one that is very different from the popular version of him in vogue in many churches. Many imagine Jesus as a meek itinerant preacher whose death was the result of a misunderstanding. They assume that Jesus came to proclaim himself as the Messiah, but was rejected by the Jews who were looking for a political Messiah who would conquer Israel's enemies and restore the nation of Israel to her former glory. It is true that the word Messiah had become a loaded term with nationalistic and political overtones. Wright writes that "the term had become so loaded with the hopes of a national, political and even military, Jewish restoration that it could not carry the understanding of his messiahship which Jesus had derived from a deeper reading of his scriptures. A public proclamation of his own messiahship would have been 'heard' by his contemporaries with a load of associations that were not part of Jesus's concept of his mission."[8] But there was more to Israel's rejection of

---

8. Wright, *Knowing Jesus*, 145.

The Ninety-Sixth Thesis

Jesus than that. Jesus simply would not allow those outside of his inner circle of disciples to know who he was because they would have interfered with his plan to die on the cross for the sins of the world. Thus, the image of Jesus as a meek itinerant preacher whose death was the result of a simple misunderstanding is a false one. His death was the sole purpose of his mission. In order to ensure that the masses would not discover who he was, Jesus revealed his identity as the Messiah to a small group of disciples and then swore them to absolute secrecy. The disciples were thus insiders who knew Jesus' identity as the Messiah; everyone else was deliberately kept in the dark about this "Messianic Secret" until after Jesus had risen from the dead.

That the disciples were insiders who had been given privileged information while everyone else was kept in the dark is consistent with Jesus' peculiar explanation for why he spoke in parables. When the disciples asked Jesus why he spoke plainly to them but in parables to everyone else, Jesus gave a response that is so bizarre that it is either ignored by churches or read quickly and passed over without comment. Some might even hope that no one will notice what Jesus said.

> He told them, "The secret of the kingdom of God has been given to you. But to those on the outside everything is said in parables *so that, 'they may be ever seeing but never perceiving, and ever hearing but never understanding; otherwise they might turn and be forgiven!'"* (Mark 4:11–12).[9]

Matthew's account is a little more expansive, but just as shocking. It reads:

> He replied, "The knowledge of the secrets of the kingdom of heaven has been given to you, but not to them. Whoever has will be given more, and he will have an abundance. Whoever does not have, even what he has will be taken from him. *This is why I speak to them in parables: 'Though seeing, they do not see; though hearing, they do not hear or understand.'* In them is fulfilled the prophecy of Isaiah: 'You will be ever hearing but never understanding; you

---

9. I do not want to get too technical with Greek grammar, but the controversy surrounds the Greek word translated "so that," which implies that Jesus speaks in parables *so that* the masses will not understand. Cranfield gives a nice summary of all the options available to the translator (Cranfield, *Mark*, 155–57), but most of these are nothing but attempts to soften the plain meaning of Jesus' words. Cranfield knows this and writes that if the Greek word translated *so that* is given its proper final force, "its significance is that the fact that the secret of the kingdom of God, in accordance with O.T. prophecy, remains hidden from many is something that is within the purpose of God" (*Mark*, 156)!

The Messianic Secret

will be ever seeing but never perceiving. For this people's heart has become calloused; they hardly hear with their ears, and they have closed their eyes. Otherwise they might see with their eyes, hear with their ears, understand with their hearts and turn, and I would heal them.' But blessed are your eyes because they see, and your ears because they hear" (Matt 13:11–16).[10]

Why did Jesus speak plainly to the disciples, but in strange parables to the masses? Because "the knowledge of the secrets of the kingdom of heaven have been given to you [the disciples], but not to them [the masses]" (Matt 13:11). Jesus spoke in parables so that the masses would not understand (Mark 4:11–12)! Why have I never heard this in a church sermon? The disciples were among the privileged few to whom was revealed the knowledge that Jesus was the Messiah.[11] Everyone else had to be kept in the dark about this secret until after Jesus' death and resurrection because only then would Jesus' mission have been accomplished.

The observation that Jesus came to earth with a very specific plan is interesting not only for its intrinsic value, but also for what it teaches us about God who also has a plan. It is the thesis of the paragraphs that follow that Jesus' plan can be used as a model to give us insight into God's plan and to help us understand God's role in the world today.

The first and most important observation is that Jesus had a plan and absolutely nothing was allowed to interfere with that plan. In order to make sense of God then, we must understand that he too has a plan and absolutely nothing can be allowed to interfere with it. Understanding this is the first step toward a proper understanding of God.

---

10. This passage of Isaiah quoted here by Matthew is also quoted in the book of John, where there is an unexpected twist: God is said to be the one who has blinded the masses' eyes and hardened their hearts. John 12:37–40 reads: Even after Jesus had done all these miraculous signs in their presence, they still would not believe in him. This was to fulfill the word of Isaiah the prophet: "Lord, who has believed our message and to whom has the arm of the Lord been revealed?" For this reason they could not believe, because, as Isaiah says elsewhere: "He has blinded their eyes and deadened their hearts, so they can neither see with their eyes, nor understand with their hearts, nor turn—and I would heal them." In another passage Jesus says: "For judgment I have come into this world, so that the blind will see and those who see will become blind" (John 9:39). But all of this was done with the best of intentions, namely to make sure that Jesus' plan to die on the cross for the sins of the world would not be thwarted.

11. That the disciples saw themselves as insiders with privileged information is also supported by John 14:22. In this verse, Judas (not Iscariot) asked Jesus, "Why do you intend to show yourself to us and not to the world?"

The Ninety-Sixth Thesis

Second, although Jesus was the son of God, and thus all powerful, his powers were limited when he was on earth. He freely admitted that he did not know everything. For example, when the woman who had been subject to bleeding for twelve years secretly touched Jesus, he did not know who touched him (Mark 5:25–34). He also admitted that he had no knowledge of when he would return to earth (Matt 24:36). But Jesus' limitations extended beyond knowledge. For example, he did not heal everyone, but only a fraction of all those who needed healing. Even though Jesus was God and could theoretically have healed anyone, something prevented him from doing all the good that he as a good God would otherwise have wanted to do. Identifying what this was is the key to unlocking some of the most perplexing mysteries of God.

Interestingly, like Jesus, God the Father, appears to have limitations. Who has not asked where God is in times of trouble? Who has not asked why God permits evil? Something is preventing God from doing all the good that we would otherwise expect him to do. But here is the problem. God, by definition, is all powerful and should not have any limitations. If he has limitations, then he is not all powerful and, thus, not divine. However, there is one thing that could prevent a good, all-powerful God from doing all the good he would otherwise want to do that would not detract at all from his omnipotence. The clue to solving this riddle is found in Jesus.

Why did Jesus not want everyone to know that he was the Messiah? Why did Jesus not heal everyone? Why did Jesus not help everyone who needed him? Why did Jesus not abolish all evil and immediately set up his kingdom? Because doing these things would have interfered with his plan to die on the cross for the sins of the world. Jesus had a plan and every action and inaction was subordinate to that plan. He could not do anything that would jeopardize his plan. This is the clue we have been searching for. Jesus was limited not by his power, but by his plan. It was his plan that prevented him from doing all the good that he would otherwise have wanted to do. This observation applies equally to God who also has a plan. Why does God not reveal himself in an undeniable way? Why does God not get more involved in the world's affairs? Why does God not eliminate evil? Because doing these things would interfere with his plan. Although God is all powerful and can do anything he wants, he cannot do anything that will compromise his plan. In the Lord's prayer, Jesus taught his disciples to pray "Thy will be done" (Matt 6:10). What exactly does this mean? It means if it is in accordance with your plan. Thus, what is the one thing that could prevent a good, all-powerful God from doing all the good that he would otherwise want to do that would not detract at all from his omnipotence? We now have the answer we have been searching for; the answer is his plan!

The observation that God has a plan and that it is his plan that prevents him from doing all the good that he would otherwise want to do helps us to better understand God, who so often seems impersonal. God's lack of involvement in the world is often interpreted as a sign that he either does not exist, or that he is elusive and indifferent. The reality is that he is not elusive and indifferent at all. What we must understand is that there is a reason why he cannot be more involved than he is and that is that he has a plan and he is sticking to it. Understanding this helps us to resolve the age-old debate regarding theism and deism.

There has long been a debate about whether God is theistic or deistic. According to the theistic model, God is intimately and actively involved in the affairs of the world. According to the deistic model, God does not get involved in the affairs of the world at all. Although God created the world, he wound it up like a clock and lets it run its course.

Both the theistic and deistic models have their advantages and disadvantages. An advantage of the theistic model is that it corresponds with the Bible, which teaches that God is intimately and actively involved in the affairs of the world. A disadvantage of the theistic model is that it is hard to reconcile with the problem of evil. Why would a good, all-powerful God not simply vanquish all evil? An advantage of the deistic model is that it is perceived to be more compatible with the problem of evil. There is a God who is all powerful; however, he is impersonal and uninterested in the affairs of man. A problem with the deistic model is that it does not explain why God would create humans only to be uninterested in them. The question is, which of these models best represents God?

On a superficial level, it may seem that the theistic and deistic models are mutually exclusive. After all, how can God be both loving and involved and, at the same time, aloof and indifferent? However, when Jesus was on earth, there were times when he was intimately and actively involved in the affairs of the world (theistic), such as when he healed people, and times when he showed signs of indifference and not wanting to be involved at all (deistic), such as when he chose not to heal people. To some he must have appeared friendly and warm, while to others he must have appeared aloof and indifferent.[12] For example, when the Syro-Phoenician (a non-Jewish)

---

12. When reading the Bible, the reader must read between the lines. In Matt 26:11,

The Ninety-Sixth Thesis

woman asked Jesus to heal her daughter, Jesus responded to her coldly, saying: "I was sent only to the lost sheep of Israel" (Matt 15:24).[13] That this was not an isolated incident is indicated from other passages, including those that show Jesus ignoring shouts of help from the crowds.[14] Thus, in the same Jesus we find two seemingly contradictory sides that correspond with both of our models. Is it possible then that these models for understanding God are not mutually exclusive, but are equally representative of the one true God?

Like Jesus, there are times when God is intimately and actively involved in the affairs of the world and times when he is not. The Bible attests to this. The Bible tells stories that span hundreds and even thousands of years. Because the biblical writers naturally selected stories that highlighted God's involvement in the world, it is easy for readers to get a skewed impression and conclude that the miraculous was much more common in biblical times than it really was. The truth is that God's direct involvement in the world has always been the exception, not the rule. For example, during the four hundred years that the children of Israel were slaves in Egypt, there were no miracles or any other visible signs of God's power. To those

---

Jesus said, "The poor you will always have with you." This was a tacit admission that when it came to poverty, he was not getting involved. Of course, he had the power to eliminate poverty, but that was not part of his plan, at least not at that time.

13. At first Jesus tried to ignore her. The Greek literally reads: "But he did not answer a word to her" (author's translation). Only after the disciples became annoyed with her persistent cries for help did Jesus stop to talk with her (Matt 15:23–28). Jesus then tried to dismiss her and said: "It is not right to take the children's bread and toss it to their dogs" (Matt 15:26). In other words, it is not right to take what belongs to the Jews and give it to Gentiles. The woman responded, "But even the dogs eat the crumbs that fall from their masters' table" (Matt 15:27). Only after hearing of her great faith did Jesus heal the woman's daughter (Mat 15:28).

14. In Matt 10:5–8 Jesus told the disciples, "Do not go among the Gentiles or enter any town of the Samaritans. Go rather to the lost sheep of Israel. As you go, preach this message: 'The kingdom of heaven is near. Heal the sick, raise the dead, cleanse those who have leprosy, drive out demons.'" In other words, do not perform miracles among the Gentiles or Samaritans, but only among the children of Israel! When it came to non-Jews, Jesus' plan required that he generally not get involved. Similarly, as word spread about Jesus and his miracles, it was only natural that he had to ignore at least some shouts of help from the crowds. Several New Testament stories allude to this, including the story of the healing of the two blind men (Matt 9:27–33). In this story, two blind men followed Jesus crying out for mercy. That they had been ignored for some time is indicated not only by the present tense of the Greek verbs, which indicates a continuous crying out, but also by the fact that Jesus did not immediately heal them, but only did so after they had followed him into the house (Matt 9:28–30).

The Messianic Secret

generations God must have seemed like a deistic God, uninterested in their affairs. However, to that generation that God delivered from bondage at the end of the four-hundred-year period God was not aloof and indifferent at all, but rather a theistic God who was intimately and actively involved in their personal affairs.[15] The same observation applies equally today. There are some—perhaps the majority—who go through life without any awareness of God's power, but then there are others who are equally confident that God has been intimately involved in their personal affairs. Clearly then the theistic and deistic models are not mutually exclusive, but are equally representative of the one true God.

The argument that God is not only a theistic God, but also a deistic God is also supported by the presence of criminal laws in the Old Testament. These laws deal with how criminals are to be punished. The presence of these laws is a subtle confession that God generally does not get involved in the affairs of the world. After all, there would be no need for such laws if God were going to intervene and stop criminal activity before it happened!

Some Christians might take offense to the idea that God is deistic as well as theistic. But such offense is unwarranted because the difference is merely a matter of perspective. Contrary to classical deism, God's lack of involvement in the world should not be taken to mean that he does not care, only that from our perspective it often seems that way. He obviously does care or he would never get involved at all. His lack of involvement has more to do with his plan, which requires that he generally allow the world to run its course. But why would God's plan require that he generally allow the world to run its course? Once again, the answer is found in Jesus' plan.

When we look carefully at Jesus' plan, one thing that stands out is that he went out of his way to keep his identity a secret. He did not want the rank-and-file masses to know that he was the Messiah because they would have interfered with his plan to die on the cross for the sins of the world. This is a perfect parallel with God who also wants to keep his existence a secret. For some reason, God does not want it to be obvious that he exists. This is clear from the fact that he chooses not to reveal himself in an undeniable way. But why would God want to keep his existence a secret? The answer must be for the same reason that Jesus wanted to keep his identity a secret, namely because doing so would interfere with his plan. But how

---

15. He told Moses: "I have indeed seen the misery of my people in Egypt. I have heard them crying out because of their slave drivers, and I am concerned about their suffering" (Exod 3:7).

The Ninety-Sixth Thesis

would God's revelation of himself interfere with his plan? An observation from everyday life offers a constructive analogy.

I, like many, take the same route to work every day. Over the years, I have learned that I can always discern when a cop is ahead by watching the brake lights of the cars in front of me. Naturally drivers who do not want a ticket slow down when they see a cop. But this observation reveals something about human behavior and holds a clue to understanding one of the reasons why God's plan requires that he keep his existence a secret.

Humans are generally well behaved when they are under the watchful eye of an authority, but not so well behaved when they are not. The police, because they are authority figures, have a unique perspective on this. When they are out on patrol, they are surrounded by what must appear to be model citizens. Not only do all the drivers around them obey the speed limit, but very few will even attempt to pass them. If an officer turns his signal on to switch lanes, the courteous drivers slow down and nicely wave him over. But something strange happens at the end of the officer's shift when that officer gets into his or her private car to go home. A different side of human behavior is revealed. People speed and pass the officer at will. If the officer turns his signal on to switch lanes, people speed up and block him from getting over. Others cut him off and, some, even give him inappropriate hand gestures. Surely, he must wonder what happened to all the courteous drivers who were out earlier in the day when he was on patrol! This observation gives us insight into why God's plan requires that he keep his existence a secret.

God, like the police, is an authority figure. When humans slow down or drive more respectfully when they see a cop, are they obeying the law because they want to, or because they have to? Obviously, they are obeying the law because they have to in order to avoid a ticket. But is this real obedience? God in his wisdom knows that it is not. He wants people to obey him not because they have to, but because they want to. He desires an obedience that flows naturally from love. The only way for God to achieve this is to keep his existence a secret and to give humans the freedom to seek him and to learn to love him, and consequently to transform into the people that he wants them to become. The Bible says that God created man for his pleasure (Rev 4:11).[16] But what pleasure could God possibly find in us? A clue to the

---

16. Tozer writes: "God formed us for Himself. The *Shorter Catechism*, 'Agreed upon by the Reverend Assembly of Divines at Westminster,' as the old *New England Primer* has it, asks the questions *what* and *why* and answers them in one short sentence hardly matched in any uninspired work. '*Question*: What is the chief end of man? *Answer*: Man's

The Messianic Secret

answer to this question is found in the analogy above. I will return to this question in the concluding chapter. For now, it is sufficient to say that God wants people to obey him not because they have to, but because they want to. I am not sure if we can fully grasp the power of that kind of obedience, an obedience that derives from love, not from coercion.[17] If God can teach us to be trustworthy when we cannot see him, then he can certainly trust us when we can see him. There is a wisdom here that can only be described as otherworldly.

If there is one reason why people do not believe in God it is the existence of evil. The Greek philosopher Epicurus is often credited with having developed what has been called the logical argument from evil. This argument is often framed this way: There is evil in the world. God hates evil. Therefore, God does not exist. However, what this argument does not take into account is that there may be reasons why God permits evil. Surely God could vanquish all evil in an instant. The fact that he does not suggests that it plays a role in his plan. That does not mean that God created evil or that he wants it, only that he allows it and uses it to the advantage of his plan. Once again, Jesus' plan offers a constructive analogy.

We have already learned that Jesus had a plan and that it was his plan that prevented him from doing all the good that he would otherwise have wanted to do. But there is something more shocking about Jesus' plan that goes way beyond not helping everyone who needed him and that is that a certain amount of evil was an essential part of his plan.

It is well known that Jesus chose Judas Iscariot to be one of his twelve disciples and that Judas later betrayed Jesus. Some have suggested that Judas must have been a good man who later became evil because, in their minds, it does not make sense that Jesus would have intentionally chosen such a man to be one of his disciples. But that is not what the Bible teaches. On the contrary, the Bible records that Jesus chose Judas to be one of his disciples *knowing full well* that he would betray him. "For Jesus had known from the beginning which of them did not believe and who would betray

---

chief end is to glorify God and enjoy him forever.' With this agree the four and twenty elders who fall on their faces to worship Him that liveth forever and ever, saying, 'Thou art worthy, O Lord, to receive glory and honour and power: for thou hast created all things, and *for thy pleasure they are and were created*' (Revelation 4:11)" (*Pursuit of God*, 32).

17. Cranfield writes something very similar to this when he notes that repentance is made possible by the inward working of the Holy Spirit, "but would be rendered impossible by the external compulsion of a manifestation of the unveiled divine majesty" (*Mark*, 158).

The Ninety-Sixth Thesis

him" (John 6:64).[18] The choice of Judas was no mistake; Judas was part of Jesus' plan![19] Jesus intentionally chose Judas to be one of his twelve disciples because Jesus' plan required that someone within his inner circle betray him and deliver him to the authorities so that he would ultimately be crucified. Thus, Jesus did not choose Judas because he was good man, but precisely because he was not a good man. Judas was evil and thus the perfect person to fulfill the role that Jesus needed him to play. We must conclude then that since a certain amount of evil was a necessary component of Jesus' plan, a certain amount of evil is also a necessary component of God's plan.[20] After all, Jesus' plan is God's plan! But why would evil be part of God's plan? Perhaps because we learn from it.

For those who pay attention, there are a lot of lessons in life. These lessons are part of what makes us wiser as we get older. One of the things that I have learned is that the world is a dangerous place and that humans are capable of unimaginable evil. However, I would never have known this if God eliminated evil. Who would have ever believed that one human's selfish ambitions would lead to the deaths of over six million Jews had God intervened and not allowed it to happen? The Bible paints man in a very negative light. Jeremiah wrote: "The heart is deceitful above all things and beyond cure. Who can understand it?"[21] By allowing history to play out with limited interference, God is teaching us valuable life lessons that reinforce biblical teachings, in this particular case that the Bible's assessment of the human heart is exactly right. God wants us to see what humans are capable of. One reason for this is because many of us would never believe it.

There is a famous photo of Adolf Hitler standing in front of the Eiffel Tower days after Germany conquered France in June of 1940. Here was man in the height of his glory. He not only had wealth and power, but his foot on the throat of Germany's arch enemy. On the day that photo was

---

18. That Jesus knew all this from the beginning is supported by other verses: "For he knew who was going to betray him, and that was why he said not every one was clean" (John 13:11). "Jesus, *knowing all that was going to happen to him*, went out and asked them, 'Who is it you want?'" (John 18:4).

19. If Judas were not part of Jesus' plan, why did Jesus not simply get rid of him and chose someone else to be one of his disciples?

20. If there is any doubt about God's willingness to use evil as part of his plan, consider the Old Testament where God puts lying spirits in the mouths of prophets (1 Kgs 22:23), or brings foreign nations from afar to punish Israel for disobedience (Isa 10:5–11). Clearly a good God can use evil to accomplish his will.

21. Jer 17:9.

taken, June 23, 1940, who could have ever imagined that less than five years later this same man who was now at the height of his glory would be hiding in his bunker contemplating his own suicide? There is a verse in the Bible that is extremely instructive: "All men are like grass, and all their glory is like the flowers of the field; the grass withers and the flowers fall, but the word of the Lord stands forever" (1 Pet 1:24–25).

These life lessons must be taken to their ultimate conclusion. If there are lessons in life, the implication is that someone is trying to teach us something.[22] Who could that be but God? By allowing history to play out with limited interference God is teaching us valuable life lessons that we would never learn if he were constantly interfering in the affairs of the world. But there is another reason why evil may be part of God's plan and that is that evil—and problems in general—are what compel us to seek God. A perfect example is what happened in America after the Second World War.

World War II was the low point of the twentieth century. However, after the war, there was a religious revival in America.[23] The war had driven people to reevaluate their lives and to seek God. Something positive came from this war that would likely never have occurred without it. Thus, we should not expect God to eliminate evil or even to resolve all of the world's problems. These are necessary components of God's plan because they force us to think about the bigger picture and motivate us to do the thing that God created us to do, namely to seek him.

Before concluding this chapter, there is one more aspect of Jesus' plan that requires attention and that is the human elements of his plan.

---

22. The idea that God is trying to teach us something is supported by the Old Testament. One of the thoughts that has long puzzled me about the Bible in general and the Old Testament in particular is the peculiar ways in which God chose to do things. Instead of using his powers to accomplish his will immediately, he chose to do things slowly over long periods of time. For example, when God wanted to deliver the Hebrew slaves from bondage in Egypt, why did his plan require that he use Moses and the ten plagues when he simply could have overwhelmed the Egyptians with one plague? Why did Moses and the Israelites have to live in the desert at all, let alone forty years, when God could have immediately given them the land of Canaan? Why did Joshua and the Israelites have to engage in battle at all when God could have overwhelmed their enemies in an instant? God was trying to teach them something, namely to love and trust him and, ultimately, to obey his laws (Deut 6:1–9). This conclusion is reinforced by the Hebrew word *torah*, which does not mean law as much as instruction. God was trying to transform them from the people that they were into the people that he wanted them to become. This same answer explains why Jesus did not set up his kingdom immediately after his resurrection. God is trying to teach us something.

23. Hudnut-Beumler, *God in the Suburbs*, 1, 37.

The Ninety-Sixth Thesis

As Christians we believe that Jesus was both human and divine because that is what the Bible teaches. Unfortunately, the human side of Jesus has been overshadowed by the church's emphasis on his deity. However, the humanity of Jesus should not be ignored. The humanity of Jesus is particularly obvious in his plan. Although Jesus was God, and thus omnipotent, he carried out his plan just like any other human would carry out a plan. For example, he kept secrets and relied on the cooperation of others (his disciples) to maintain his secret rather than using his powers to override people's ability to think and reason. Apparently, he wanted to preserve the secrecy of his identity without interfering with the free will of humans. But there was risk involved in this. The fact that Jesus kept secrets and warned the disciples to do the same suggests that there was a very real threat that his plan could have been thwarted. In order to diminish this threat, Jesus did what any human with a secret would do. He avoided answering direct questions about his identity and, on at least one occasion, was not entirely forthright about his intentions.

Because Jesus did not want the masses to discover his identity as the Messiah, he avoided answering direct questions about his identity.[24] For example, all four gospels record that Pontius Pilate directly asked Jesus if he was the king of the Jews. Some translations, such as the NIV, make it appear as if Jesus answered this question in the affirmative. The NIV records Jesus' response as: "Yes, it is as you say" (Matt 27:11; Mark 15:2). However, the original Greek is much vaguer than this. A literal translation of the Greek is: "You say."[25] The Greek is not even clear on whether this is a statement or a question. Does it mean something like "So you say" or "Are you saying this?" Whatever Jesus meant, it was certainly not a direct answer to Pilate's question. The vagueness of Jesus' response is exactly what we would expect in light of all those passages that emphasize Jesus' desire to keep his identity a secret. Jesus could not answer any direct question about his identity

---

24. Talking with Jesus must have been very frustrating at times because he often refused to answer questions directly. In fact, some of his responses to direct questions border along the lines of non sequiturs. For example, in John 14:22 one of Jesus' disciples asked him: "Lord, why do you intend to show yourself to us and not to the world?" Jesus responded by saying: "If anyone loves me he will obey my teaching. My Father will love him, and we will come to him and make our home with him" (John 14:23). Even the disciples seemed frustrated with Jesus' vagueness at times (John 16:17–18).

25. Bright writes: "It is significant that it is the unanimous witness of the Gospels that when Pilate asked him point-blank, 'Are you the King of the Jews?' his only answer was a blunt, 'You have said it' (Mark 15:2; Matt 27:11; Luke 23:3; John 18:33–37)—which, if cryptic, was certainly no denial" (*Kingdom of God*, 199).

The Messianic Secret

without jeopardizing his plan. Interestingly, the only time that Jesus publicly answered a direct question about his identity was at his trial before the Jewish Sanhedrin when he knew that an affirmative answer would lead to a charge of blasphemy and ultimately to the death sentence that was always part of his plan (Mark 14:61–64).[26] This lack of forthrightness on the part of Jesus raises an interesting and perhaps, in the eyes of some, even a sacrilegious question. Did Jesus lie by deliberately withholding information from those who asked for it?

Most of us are aware of two types of lies. There are lies of commission, where someone deliberately tells someone something that is false, and there are lies of omission, where someone avoids telling the whole truth. Did Jesus, the son of God, sin by not being entirely forthright about his identity? Before addressing this question, I want to address another, more specific, accusation that Jesus lied in the New Testament.

In John 7 Jesus' brothers challenged him to go to the Feast of Tabernacles in Judea to reveal himself to the world (John 7:1–5). Jesus then told them that he would not go to the Feast because the right time had not yet come (John 7:6–9). However, after his brothers left for the Feast, he too went, not publicly, but in secret (John 7:10). It is obvious from some of the extant Greek manuscripts of the Gospel of John that the scribes who copied them wanted to exonerate Jesus from even the appearance of lying, for some of them add the word "yet" in the text: "I am not *yet* going up to the Feast." But was this necessary? Did Jesus lie to his brothers when he went to the Feast?

The New Testament teaches that Jesus lived a life without sin (2 Cor 5:21). Thus, the accusation that Jesus lied is a serious one. However, this accusation is not as surprising as it may at first seem. The Pharisees, with their strict interpretation of Jewish law, had already accused Jesus of a number of sins, especially violating the Sabbath.[27] From their perspective, Jesus was a sinner who violated the law of Moses on multiple occasions. Jesus' response

---

26. Cranfield notes that "it was as a messianic pretender that he was actually condemned to death" (*Mark*, 78).

27. Old Testament law forbids work on the Sabbath (Exod 20:8–11). Jesus frequently healed on the Sabbath, thus arousing the ire of his contemporaries (Luke 13:10–17; John 9:1–34, et al.). Jesus' opponents took this law and others to the extreme and argued that no work should be done on the Sabbath, even if that work is to help someone in need. However, Jesus taught that this was based on man's interpretation of the law, not God's. In Jesus' interpretation of Old Testament law, it was perfectly appropriate, and even encouraged, to work on the Sabbath if someone needed help. Thus, while technically Jesus broke the law according to man's interpretation, he never broke it according to God's interpretation, and his interpretation is the only one that matters.

The Ninety-Sixth Thesis

to those accusations should give us insight into how he would respond to accusations that he lied.

When Jesus was accused of violating the Sabbath, he responded by emphasizing that doing good always overrides strict interpretation of Jewish law. For example, when he was accused of healing a man on the Sabbath, Jesus responded with the question: "If one of you has a son or an ox that falls into a well on the Sabbath day, will you not immediately pull him out?" (Luke 14:5). The obvious answer is: Of course they would! Clearly, as a Jew, Jesus observed the Sabbath. However, he taught that there are times when it is appropriate to work on the Sabbath, particularly when doing good for someone. In Jesus' view, doing good always overrides strict interpretation of Jewish law. Understanding this gives us insight into how Jesus would respond to false accusations that he lied.

When humans withhold information, they do so for selfish reasons, namely because it is advantageous for them to do so. When Jesus withheld information about his identity or was not forthright with his brothers, he did so for the most unselfish of reasons—to ensure his own violent death for the sins of the world at the cross of Calvary. Why did Jesus not want to tell his brothers that he was going to the Feast? Because he knew that the Jewish leaders were looking for an opportunity to kill him (John 7:1) and, had they known he was going to the Feast, they would have had their opportunity. Yes, Jesus came to die, but not at that time and not at the hands of bandits (John 7:6). Jesus' plan was to die on the cross for the sins of the world and absolutely nothing could be allowed to prevent that from happening. But once again, we see the human elements of Jesus' plan. Jesus was human and had to do things the way humans would to ensure that his plan would come to fruition. This included not only keeping secrets and relying on others to do the same, but also avoiding answering direct questions and, on at least this one occasion, not being entirely forthright about his intentions. Every decision was made with his broader plan in mind. He could not allow anything to interfere with his plan, which was to die on the cross for the sins of the world. This is very different from lying.

In conclusion, Jesus went out of his way to keep his miracles a secret because he did not want the masses to discover his identity as the long-anticipated Messiah. Thus, Jesus revealed himself to his disciples, but kept virtually everyone else in the dark about his identity until after he had risen from the dead. However, Jesus did not perform all of his miracles in secret.

The Messianic Secret

On at least some occasions, Jesus performed miracles in front of crowds (Matt 4:23–25; John 6:1–2). About this Cranfield writes:

> Throughout the ministry we can see these two motives (revealing and veiling) at work. On the one hand, Jesus gathers the crowds about him and teaches them, sends out the Twelve to preach, and reveals the power and compassion of God by his miracles. God's self-revelation is not to be accomplished in a corner. On the other hand, Jesus teaches the crowds indirectly by means of parables, seeks to conceal his miracles, and forbids the demoniacs to declare his identity. The two motives, both of which are necessary to the divine purpose, are constantly in tension—a fact which explains some apparent inconsistencies.[28]

This observation leads Cranfield to call God's self-revelation *veiled revelation*.[29] "God's self-revelation is veiled, in order that men may be left sufficient room in which to make a personal decision. A real turning to God or repentance . . . is made possible by the inward divine enabling of the Holy Spirit . . . , but would be rendered impossible by the external compulsion of a manifestation of the unveiled divine majesty. The revelation is veiled for the sake of man's freedom to believe."[30] This observation that Jesus performed some miracles in public and others in private is not a contradiction, but evidence of an elaborate plan that had been spun and conceived in the mind of God. It would seem that Jesus wanted to keep just enough of his miracles a secret so that it would not be obvious that he was the Messiah, but it also seems that he performed just enough miracles in public that people would at least speculate on that possibility.

The observation that Jesus had a plan and absolutely nothing was allowed to interfere with that plan informs our understanding of God who also has a plan. Just as Jesus could not allow anything to interfere with his plan, God cannot allow anything to interfere with his plan. God is limited not by his power, but by his plan. This insight clears up many of the misconceptions about God. Many assume that because God cannot be seen or that because there is evil in the world that God must not exist. But what is more likely, that there is no God and that everything that we see is simply the result of one big accident, or that there is a God and we simply do not understand him and his mysterious ways? In the next chapter, I highlight

28. Cranfield, *Mark*, 157.
29. Cranfield, *Mark*, 157.
30. Cranfield, *Mark*, 158.

The Ninety-Sixth Thesis

a little-known theme that runs through both the Old and New Testaments that is essential for not only understanding the character of God, but also for perceiving his mysterious role in the world. This theme is that the God of the Bible goes out of his way to defy human wisdom. This theme and its implications are the subjects of the next chapter.

Chapter 4

The God Who Defies Human Wisdom

IN THE PRECEDING CHAPTER, we learned that Jesus' plan can be used as a model to help us understand God's plan. We also learned that some of the least-known details of Jesus' life are important pieces of a puzzle that must not be ignored if we are going to understand not only Jesus, but also God and his role in the world today. But can we dig any further? Can we discern anything else about God and his plan? In this chapter, I focus on one aspect of God that gets very little attention, but is foundational for understanding who he is and how he works in the world today and that is that he reveals himself as a God who thinks and acts in defiance of human wisdom.

People today have a lot of confidence in human wisdom, and with good reason. We have put man on the moon. We can travel across the world in less than a day. And we have witnessed advancements in medicine and technology that would have seemed like science fiction just a few years ago. I have often wondered how the ancients would react if we could go back in time and tell them about the modern world. There would not even be vocabulary available to explain everyday concepts such as heating and air conditioning. Imagine trying to tell them that we have walls that blow cool and warm air! Imagine looking up at the sky and trying to tell them that we mounted a bird-like object and landed on the moon! They would no doubt conclude that someone has been smoking *hashish*! The truth is that the things we have witnessed in the modern world would seem every bit as silly to them as some of the biblical stories seem to us. This should serve as a warning to everyone; we really do not know what is or is not possible because we judge everything by our experience. This is extremely dangerous not only because our experience is limited, but also because it makes us vulnerable to a trap, a trap set by the God of the Bible who promises to defy human wisdom.

In Isa 55:8–9 the Lord says:

> "For my thoughts are not your thoughts, neither are your ways my ways," declares the LORD. "As the heavens are higher than the earth, so are my ways higher than your ways and my thoughts than your thoughts."

To say that God thinks and acts differently than humans is a truism that, at first, does not seem to require further elaboration. After all, if God exists, it is only natural that his thoughts and ways are higher than man's. But we need to probe deeper into this subject and ask, in what way are God's thoughts and ways higher than man's? Since we do not know anything about God other than what he has revealed about himself in the Bible, the only way to discern how his thoughts and ways differ from ours is by reading the Bible to gain insight into how he worked in the past. When this is done, an interesting observation comes to light.

A careful reading of the entire Bible reveals a theme that is easily overlooked when reading individual narratives. This theme is that the God of the Bible thinks and acts in defiance of human wisdom. In many instances, God does the opposite of what humans would do. In this chapter, I highlight a number of examples of this theme from both the Old and New Testaments and then discuss its implications for understanding God and his role in the world today.

It is often said that God works in mysterious ways. One reason for this is that the Bible reveals God accomplishing his will in ways that are peculiar to man and that defy conventional wisdom. One of the first examples of this is in the Old Testament story of Abram. Abram is introduced in Gen 12:1–3, where God tells him to leave his family and his country to go to a new land that God will show him. God then told Abram that God had a plan to bless all people on earth through him and his descendants. It is impossible to understand the Bible without understanding the significance of this promise. Thus, some knowledge of the broader context of the early chapters of Genesis is required.

The Bible begins with the story of creation in Genesis 1–2. God created a perfect world. There was no death, sickness or evil. God intended for

The God Who Defies Human Wisdom

man to live forever in a beautiful garden called Eden.[1] It was in this garden where God and man would have intimate fellowship and walk in harmony with one another. But something tragic happened. The man and woman God created sinned and brought a terrible curse upon the world that resulted in sin and death (Gen 3). It is no coincidence that immediately after this event, the Bible records a number of tragic stories in rapid succession (Gen 4–11). In Genesis 4, one of the sons of the first human couple killed his brother. In Genesis 5, death began taking the lives of Adam and his descendants. As years passed and man's wickedness only increased (Gen 6:5–6), God became sorry that he had made man and sent a terrible flood to eradicate the human race (Gen 6–8). By preserving the lives of Noah and his family in the ark, God was in effect starting over, hoping for better results the second time. However, the story that immediately follows the flood narrative makes it clear that the flood did little to purge the stain of sin from the human heart. In Genesis 9, Ham shamed his father Noah by looking upon him in his nakedness.[2] Finally, the unit of Genesis 4–11 closes with a story of mankind's hubris in which they build a tower to reach the heavens to make a great name for themselves (Gen 11). The central theme of Genesis 4–11 is that the world is under a terrible curse. At the end of ch. 11, one is left only to wonder if there is any way to reverse the curse. It is at this point in the book of Genesis that the Bible introduces Abram, the man who is God's solution to this curse.

Gen 12:1–3 introduces Abram with these words:

> The LORD had said to Abram, "Leave your country, your people and your father's household and go to the land I will show you. I will make you into a great nation and I will bless you; I will make your name great, and you will be a blessing. I will bless those who bless you, and whoever curses you I will curse; and all peoples on earth will be blessed through you."

---

1. There can be no doubt that, at least in the mind of the author of Genesis, Eden was a real place, because the writer puts its location near two well-known rivers, the Tigris and the Euphrates. Thus, the location of Eden would have been in Mesopotamia, somewhere in or near modern Iraq. For a discussion on the possible locations of Eden, see Beitzel, *Moody Atlas of Bible Lands*, 74–75.

2. The importance of this event cannot be overstated. After Ham shamed his drunken father by looking upon him in his nakedness, Noah awoke and put a curse not on Ham but on Ham's son, Canaan (Gen 9:25). Why is this significant? Because the inhabitants of Israel before the Hebrews took that land were called Canaanites and their land was called Canaan (Gen 12:5–6). The curse of Noah plays out later in the book of Joshua when the Hebrews expel the Canaanites from their land (see Josh 5:1; 7:9; 9:1—Judg 1).

The Ninety-Sixth Thesis

In this brief passage, God came to Abram and told him to leave his country and his family to go to a new land that God will show him. This new land was the land of Canaan which eventually became the land of Israel. God then made seven very specific promises to Abram:[3] First, God promised to make Abram into a great nation.[4] Second, God promised to *bless* him. Third, God promised to make Abram's name great (or renown) so that he would be a *blessing*. Fourth, God promised that Abram and his seed would be a *blessing* to others. Fifth, God promised to *bless* those who *bless* Abram. Sixth, God promised to curse those who curse Abram. Seventh, and most importantly, God promised that all people on earth will be *blessed* through Abram.

The word "blessing" occurs repeatedly in these verses and is obviously significant. God put a curse on the world in Genesis 3 that resulted in sin and death (Gen 4–11). However, here with the introduction of Abram, God no longer speaks of cursing but of blessing. The recurrence of the word blessing in these verses is no coincidence, but rather a literary cue that God indeed has a solution to the curse and that solution has something to do with Abram.

These verses do not explain how Abram is the solution to the curse, only that he is. The reader must assume that this will be explained in the chapters that follow. That Abram is the solution to the curse is most clearly articulated in the climactic promise that comes at the end: "All peoples on earth will be *blessed* through you" (Gen 12:3). God is going to reverse the curse by "blessing" all people through Abram and his descendants, the Jewish people (Gen 12:3). However, there is a significant problem and it is this problem that introduces the theme of God's defiance of human wisdom.

Obviously if God is going to make Abram into a great nation (Gen 12:2), Abram must first have a child. This promise is laid out in Gen 12:7, where God tells Abram: "To your *seed* [descendants] I will give this land." However, at the time of these promises, Abram is seventy-five years old and his wife is sixty-five (Gen 12:4; Gen 17:17). Thus, God's promises to Abram are entirely contingent upon the unrealistic possibility of a

---

3. There are actually eight promises if we include Gen 12:7. It states that God will give the land of Canaan (Israel) to Abram and to his seed. The separation of the eighth promise from the others marks the seventh promise as the climactic promise. Kaiser writes: "The seventh of these eight promises became the one that was emphasized, for it always appears in the climactic position, even though it was repeated to Abraham three times and once each to Isaac and Jacob (Gen 12:3; 18:18; 22:18; 26:4; 28:14)" (*Messiah*, 46–47).

4. The nation alluded to here is Israel.

The God Who Defies Human Wisdom

sixty-five-year-old woman giving birth! The question is, why would God make promises to Abram that are contingent upon something that everyone would immediately know is virtually impossible?

From a human perspective, the odds of Sarai giving birth at the age of sixty-five were already remote, but as if to defy human wisdom even more, God made Abram and Sarai wait twenty-five more years before giving them the child he had promised! During this twenty-five-year interval, even Abram and Sarai began to entertain doubts about God's ability to fulfill his promise (Gen 16:1–2; Gen 17:17–19; 18:11–12). I will explain this story in greater detail in the chapter that follows. For now, I want to focus on God's fulfillment of his promise. After twenty-five long years, God finally fulfilled his promise to Abram and gave him a son named Isaac. Human wisdom said that a sixty-five-year-old woman could not give birth and God defied that wisdom by making a ninety-year-old woman give birth (Gen 21:1–5)![5] The point of this story, and others like it, is one and the same: Nothing is impossible for God!

There will of course be some who immediately dismiss this or any other story in the Bible that contains any hint of the miraculous. However, it is important to make three observations here. First, whether one believes these stories or not, someone wrote them for others to believe. But this raises an important question. If these stories were simply invented, why did those who wrote them make them so unbelievable? Would it not have served their interests better to make them more believable by eliminating any hint of the miraculous? The fact that they passed these stories on the way they did with no apology for the miraculous makes me take these stories much more seriously.

Second, although it is true that there are stories in the Bible that strain credulity, all these stories suddenly become more credible when God is thrown into the equation. Every philosopher knows that if an all-powerful being such as God exists, then anything is possible, including the miraculous. It seems to me that the entire Bible is really about one question: Do you believe that the arm of the Lord is too short? Is anything impossible for God? Each reader must decide the answer to this question him or herself.[6]

---

5. If we listen carefully, it is almost possible to hear echoes of God's future plan for the virgin birth of the Messiah.

6. It does not follow from this conclusion that everything in the Bible has to be interpreted literally. There are some very sincere Christians who believe that at least some of the biblical stories were told to teach lessons, much like Jesus' parables. It is important to be open-minded to other perspectives. No one knows for sure what did or did not

The Ninety-Sixth Thesis

Third, it is important to discern what God is doing in this story, and others like it, and that is that he is revealing himself as a God who acts in direct defiance of human wisdom. Humans say that a sixty-five-year-old woman cannot give birth and God defies that wisdom by making a ninety-year-old woman give birth! Understanding that God acts in direct defiance of human wisdom makes all these stories that seem so unlikely from a human perspective all the more plausible. It would be just like the God of the Bible to want humans in their hubris to doubt him and his power so that he can one day defy so-called human wisdom. Humans, it would seem, are in danger of being baited into a trap of their own arrogance and it is the God who defies human wisdom who has set the bait.

There are at least two ways that God defies human wisdom in the Bible. Sometimes God defies human wisdom by doing things in unexpected ways, such as when Abraham and Sarah gave birth in their old age.[7] On other occasions, God defies human wisdom by accomplishing his will through weak and ineffectual individuals. These are the kinds of things that we must look for not only when reading the Bible, but also in life in general because the same God still works mysteriously in the world today.

In Old Testament times it was a well-established custom that the oldest son had privileges unavailable to the other children, including a greater share of the family inheritance (Deut 21:17). When Abraham's son Isaac and his wife Rebekah gave birth to Esau and Jacob it was an expectation that Esau would be granted the rights of the firstborn. However, in defiance of both human wisdom and conventions, God chose to bless the younger son Jacob rather than his brother Esau (Gen 25:23). This rejection of the prerogatives of the firstborn in favor of another son is another theme in the book of Genesis. God not only chose Jacob over Esau, but also Perez over Zerah (Gen 38:27–30), Ephraim over Manasseh (Gen 48:10–20), and Judah over Reuben (Gen 49:3–4, 8–12). When Jacob put his right hand on Ephraim and his left hand on Manasseh, Joseph immediately recognized that this was not according to convention and tried to stop his aged father from blessing the younger son over the older one, but Jacob dismissed Joseph's attempt and said only: "I know, my son, I know. He too will become

---

happen in the past. However, because the God of the Bible reveals himself as a God who defies human wisdom, I would be very careful about drawing conclusions about what did or did not happen in the past. If God could raise Christ from the dead, why should we think that anything is impossible for him?

7. God eventually changed Abram's name to Abraham (Gen 17:5) and Sarai's name to Sarah (Gen 17:15).

a people, and he too will become great. Nevertheless, his younger brother will be greater than he, and his descendants will become a group of nations" (Gen 48:19). The message should be clear: God does things according to his wisdom, not according to human convention.

God's choice of Jacob over Esau is noteworthy for another reason. The book of Genesis paints Jacob in a particularly negative light. Jacob is a flawed character who is best known for having stolen both his brother's birthright (Gen 25:29–34) and his blessing (Gen 27). Human wisdom would lead many to conclude that such a man would immediately be disqualified from God's service. Nevertheless, God chose Jacob over his brother Esau (Mal 1:2–3).

The theme of God's defiance of human wisdom continues in the book of Exodus, where it is revealed that the person God had chosen to lead the children of Israel had an uncharacteristic flaw. When humans choose a leader, it is an expectation that he or she be an effective communicator. But when God chose Moses to lead the children of Israel, he chose a man with a speech problem. Moses used this weakness as an excuse to disqualify himself from God's service. "O Lord, I have never been eloquent, neither in the past nor since you have spoken to your servant. I am slow of speech and tongue" (Exod 4:10). Others made similar excuses for why they did not qualify for God's service. Gideon tried to disqualify himself on the grounds that his clan was the weakest in Manasseh and that he was the least in his family (Judg 6:15).[8] Jeremiah tried to disqualify himself on the grounds that he was only a boy and did not yet know how to speak (Jer 1:6). But what they did not know was that all the things that would normally disqualify a person from human service are the very things that qualify a person for God's service. The reason for this is obvious: When someone who is qualified accomplishes an amazing feat, they get the glory, but when God uses the weak to accomplish his will, he gets the glory.

God's defiance of human wisdom is also manifest in the story of Gideon in which God tells Gideon that he has too many men to fight the numerically superior Midianites. God then reduced Gideon's army from thirty-two thousand men to three hundred men and then used those inferior forces to defeat the vastly more numerous Midianites (Judg 7:1–7)! The reason for this reduction is very insightful: The LORD said to Gideon, "You have too

---

8. Saul, Israel's first king, said something similar to this when Samuel told him that he was to be Israel's first king: "But am I not a Benjamite, from the smallest tribe of Israel, and is not my clan the least of all the clans of the tribe of Benjamin?" (1 Sam 9:21).

many men for me to deliver Midian into their hands. In order that Israel may not boast against me that her own strength has saved her" (Judg 7:2).

This was not the only time that God used an outnumbered army to defeat a numerically superior army. Years earlier in the days of Abram, God took Abram and the 318 men who were allied with him and used them to defeat the mighty kings of the east and their armies (Gen 14:1–17). Years later, in the days of King Ahab, Israel was in battle against the Arameans. The book of Kings describes the Israelite camp as two small flocks of goats, while the Arameans covered the entire countryside (1 Kgs 20:27). Human wisdom would have immediately concluded that Israel stood no chance and under normal circumstances human wisdom would have been right. Nevertheless, Israel was ultimately victorious because the God who defies human wisdom was on Israel's side (1 Kgs 20:29–30).

The theme of God's defiance of human wisdom is also present in God's choice of David as Israel's king. When Samuel was dispatched to anoint one of Jesse's sons as king, Samuel looked at the largest, Eliab, and immediately concluded that he must be the one whom God has chosen (1 Sam 16:6). But Samuel's judgment was based on human wisdom, not on the wisdom of God. The Lord told Samuel: "Do not consider his appearance or his height, for I have rejected him. The LORD does not look at the things man looks at. Man looks at the outward appearance, but the LORD looks at the heart" (1 Sam 16:7). When Samuel finally understood this, he rejected all the other, more capable, sons of Jesse and anointed the youngest, David, to be Israel's next king (1 Sam 16:11–13).

When the Philistine giant, Goliath, taunted the armies of God, there were many experienced soldiers God could have chosen to fight the Philistine, including any of David's three older and much larger brothers (1 Sam 16:6–7; 17:12–14, 33). But that is how humans do things, not how God does them. In defiance of human wisdom, God chose David, the youngest and presumably the smallest of Jesse's sons, to defeat the mighty Goliath (1 Sam 17:33, 38–39, 48–50).

God's defiance of human wisdom is also manifest in the story of Elijah, the prophet to whom God revealed himself in a strange and unexpected way (1 Kgs 19:11–12). At least since the experience of Mt. Sinai (Exod 19:16–19), God had been associated with such dreadful phenomena as the storm, earthquake, and fire.[9] But contrary to what Elijah had thought, God is also associated with phenomena as insignificant and imperceptible as

---

9. Keil and Delitzsch, *Kings and Chronicles*, 182.

The God Who Defies Human Wisdom

the sound of a gentle breeze. God wanted Elijah to know that he is always present and that his hand often moves imperceptibly in the world.

After Solomon's temple had been destroyed and the inhabitants of Judah had been taken into exile (586 BC), the prophets who had warned of the coming destruction of Judah wrote about a time of restoration when God's people would return from exile and rebuild the temple. When the exiles eventually returned to Judah, they faced a lot of setbacks rebuilding it. The book of Nehemiah records some of the problems faced by those who rebuilt it.[10] God then told Zerubbabel through the prophet Zechariah that the completion of the temple would be carried out not according to human wisdom, but according to the Spirit of God: "Not by might nor by power, but by my Spirit" (Zech 4:6).

The theme of God's defiance of human wisdom is not limited to the Old Testament, but is also woven into the tapestry of the New Testament. It is well known that the children of earthly kings live lives of privilege. Ironically, Jesus was not just a son of a king but *the Son of the King of the entire universe*. If anyone could have expected a life of privilege, it should have been Jesus. But contrary to human wisdom, God's son was not born with all the pomp and celebration of a child of royal birth, but outside in a stable, surrounded by filthy animals (Luke 2:1–7).

Before Jesus was born into this world, God could have selected any family to raise his son. Human wisdom would lead many to assume that God would choose not only a good family to raise his son, but also a wealthy family who could provide for all Jesus' needs. But once again, contrary to human wisdom, God did exactly the opposite and chose a poor family to raise his son.[11]

Similarly, God could have chosen one of the great cities for his royal son's birth. The most obvious choice would have been Jerusalem, the city of the great king David. But again, in defiance of human wisdom, Jesus was not born in Jerusalem or in any other city of significance, but rather in the small and insignificant town of Bethlehem. Hundreds of years before Jesus was born, the Old Testament prophet Micah had written about a ruler who would one day come from this small and insignificant town: "But you, Bethlehem Ephrathah, though you are *small* among the clans of Judah, out

---

10. Nehemiah 4 records not only how the enemies of the Jews tried to prevent them from rebuilding the temple, but also how they planned to kill them (Neh 4:1–11).

11. We know that Jesus' family was of limited means because of the offering his parents made at the temple at the time of his birth (Luke 2:24). The offering of a pair of turtle doves or pigeons was the most modest of offerings reserved for the very poor (Lev 12:8).

of you will come for me one who will be ruler over Israel, whose origins are from of old, from ancient times" (Mic 5:2).

If Jesus was not born in a great city, human wisdom might expect that he would at least be raised in a great city. But Jesus was not raised in Jerusalem or in any other city of prominence. On the contrary, he was raised in the lowly city of Nazareth, a place so despised that Nathaniel could ask: "Nazareth! Can anything good come from there?" (John 1:46).[12]

After his baptism, Jesus choose twelve men to be his disciples (Mark 1:14–20; 3:13–19). Human wisdom would naturally choose from among the prominent members of society, men of wealth, power, and political influence. But, as we have seen so often, that which is in accordance with human wisdom runs counter to the wisdom of God. It should be no surprise that the men Jesus chose to be his disciples were for the most part men of insignificance. The book of Acts refers to some of them as "unschooled, ordinary men" (Acts 4:13).

God's defiance of human wisdom is perhaps nowhere more obvious than in Jesus' teachings. In both the Sermon of the Mount (Matt 5–7) and the Sermon of the Plain (Luke 6), Jesus takes the conventional wisdom of this world and turns it on its head. In the kingdom of this world, it is the wealthy and those with political power who are considered blessed. But in the kingdom of God, it is the poor, those who hunger, weep, and those persecuted because of their faith who are considered blessed (Luke 6:20–22).

In the kingdom of this world, if someone strikes you on the cheek, you strike him back. But in God's kingdom, when someone strikes you on the cheek, you turn and allow him to strike the other as well (Matt 5:39). In the kingdom of this world, if someone hates you, you hate him back. But in God's kingdom you love your enemies and pray for God's blessing upon them (Matt 5:44). In the kingdom of this world, people pray and give alms in order to be seen by men (Matt 6:1–2, 5), but in God's kingdom such things are done in complete secrecy (Matt 6:1–8).

In the kingdom of this world, greatness is often defined by money and power. But in God's kingdom, there is a different standard of greatness where it is the lowly servant and the one who humbles himself like a little child who is the greatest (Mark 10:42–45; Matt 18:1–4). This lesson was difficult for Jesus' disciples to grasp, as is obvious from the fact that some

---

12. Interestingly, Wittenberg, Germany, was also considered an insignificant place until Luther made it famous. Pettegree notes: "Indeed, one of the reasons opponents so underestimated Luther at first was because they simply could not conceive anything of importance emerging from such a place" (*Brand Luther*, 8).

The God Who Defies Human Wisdom

of them were concerned with who among them would be the greatest in God's kingdom (Luke 9:46). Jesus then took a little child and had him stand beside him and told his disciples that it is the least among them who is the greatest (Luke 9:48).

In the kingdom of this world, rulers are here to be served, but in God's kingdom it is the king of all the universe who is here to serve (Matt 20:28). This was the point that Jesus tried to make when he got down on his knees, removed his robe, and washed his disciple's feet (John 13:1-17). No human of any significance would ever consider performing such a lowly task, but such is the way of the king of the universe, who operates on a plane unfamiliar to man.

It has been said that you can tell the measure of a man by how he treats those who cannot do anything for him. Observations like this are very much in line with the teachings of Jesus. Jesus said: "When you give a luncheon or dinner, do not invite your friends, your brothers or relatives, or your rich neighbors; if you do, they may invite you back and so you will be repaid. But when you give a banquet, invite the poor, the crippled, the lame, the blind, and you will be blessed. Although they cannot repay you, you will be repaid at the resurrection of the righteous" (Luke 14:12-14).

When I was a child, my uncle and aunt had an annual Christmas Eve party at their beautiful home. These parties were a lot of fun and some of my fondest memories are from these gatherings. Looking back, there is one thing in particular that stands out to me about these parties and that is that there were a number of years when my uncle and aunt invited the town vagrant. Although I am not sure if he slept on the streets, I know he was very poor. He certainly did not have a job. All day long he walked the streets and was dressed like any other homeless vagrant. But at these parties, he was always dressed neatly and I am sure my uncle either bought him a sweater or gave him one of his own. Today I cannot help but think how their invitation to this lonely and poor man was very much in line with Jesus' teaching alluded to in the paragraph above.

When Jesus was criticized for spending time with tax collectors and sinners, Jesus responded by saying: "It is not the healthy who need a doctor, but the sick. I have not come to call the righteous, but sinners" (Mark 2:17). God's defiance of human wisdom is manifest in this: while Jesus spent time with prostitutes, tax collectors, and sinners, he reserved his harshest criticism for the religious leaders of his day who, in his view, were in danger of not even entering the kingdom of God (Matt 5:20). How angry they must have been when Jesus told them: "I tell you the truth, the tax collectors and the prostitutes are entering the kingdom of God ahead of you!"[13] It is very likely that even today Jesus' sharpest criticism would be reserved for those of us who profess his name.

Jesus did not talk like anyone else. He spoke with authority and said things that, at first, must have sounded like nonsense, but with more reflection made perfect sense. He said: "Woe to you when all men speak well of you, for that is how their fathers treated the false prophets" (Luke 6:26). Why would it be a problem if everyone speaks well of someone? The Old Testament prophets offer a constructive analogy. In Old Testament times, there were both true and false prophets. The former spoke for God and told the king and people what they did not want to hear. The latter did not speak for God and told the king and people what they wanted to hear. Naturally, the false prophets were much more popular.[14] Popular messages may make one popular with men, but they are unlikely to derive from God. If all people speak well of you, then it is very likely you are more concerned with pleasing men than with pleasing God. You cannot please both! I will return to this topic in the concluding chapter because it seems to me that we have here a very important method for evaluating not only the claims of true and false prophets today, but also the competing truth claims of the various religions.

The crucifixion of Jesus is perhaps the fullest expression of God's defiance of human wisdom. Earlier we learned that only Jesus was responsible for his rejection by the Jews. He simply would not allow them to know that he was the Messiah. But there was another reason for their rejection of Jesus and that is that he simply was not what they had anticipated. When people thought of the end of the age and the coming of the Messiah, they thought in political terms of a conquering Messiah who would come and overwhelm his enemies. They simply could not have imagined that there was any kind of victory in what appeared to be an ignoble, common criminal's death. Cranfield writes: "In the last hours of his life his incognito

---

13. Matt 21:31.

14. A perfect example of this is God's prophet Jeremiah, who told the king and people what they did not want to hear and was punished for it. Jeremiah told the king and people to surrender to the Babylonians because this judgment was from God because of their disobedience to his law (Jer 21:1–10). Jeremiah's message sounded like treason (Jer 38:4). He was beaten, put in chains (Jer 20:1–2), and thrown into a cistern (Jer 38). However, one of the reasons his writings survived and made their way into the Bible is because his words that no one wanted to hear were eventually proven true.

The God Who Defies Human Wisdom

deepens until in the helplessness, nakedness and agony of the Cross, abandoned by God and man, he becomes the absolute antithesis of everything that the world understands by divinity and kingship."[15] Paul wrote to the Corinthian church: "For the message of the cross is foolishness to those who are perishing, but to us who are being saved it is the power of God" (1 Cor 1:18). The idea of a dying messiah who would willfully submit not only to his death but also to being beaten and spat upon by men he had created was so far removed from the minds of men that it could only have been spun and conceived in the mind of God. However, there were clues in the Old Testament that something like this would happen. Hundreds of years earlier, the Old Testament prophet Isaiah had written about a figure eerily similar to Christ: "Surely he took up our infirmities and carried our sorrows, yet we considered him stricken by God, smitten by him, and afflicted. But he was pierced for our transgressions, he was crushed for our iniquities; the punishment that brought us peace was upon him, and by his wounds we are healed. We all, like sheep, have gone astray, each of us has turned to his own way; and the Lord has laid on him the iniquity of us all" (Isa 53:4–6).

God's defiance of human wisdom also plays a prominent role in the life and teachings of the Apostle Paul. Paul is introduced as a zealous Jew who wanted nothing more than to destroy the church. He not only threw Christians in prison, but also consented to their deaths (Acts 7:57—8:1). But the God who defies wisdom had a different plan for Paul's life. One day, around noon, as Paul approached Damascus with letters from the high priest that gave him authority to arrest any Christians he found there, something happened that would forever alter the course of Paul's life.[16]

> As he neared Damascus on his journey, suddenly a light from heaven flashed around him. He fell to the ground and heard a voice say to him, "Saul, Saul, why do you persecute me?" "Who are you, Lord?" Saul asked. "I am Jesus, whom you are persecuting," he replied. "Now get up and go into the city, and you will be told what you must do." The men traveling with Saul stood there speechless; they heard the sound but did not see anyone. Saul got up from the ground, but when he opened his eyes he could see nothing. So they led him by the hand into Damascus. For three days he was blind, and did not eat or drink anything. (Acts 9:3–9)

---

15. Cranfield, *Mark*, 157.
16. Before his conversion, Paul's name was Saul.

The Ninety-Sixth Thesis

Today this Paul, who once fought so zealously against the Christian faith, is recognized not only as the greatest Christian missionary of all time, but also as the one who wrote much of the New Testament. Who but the God who defies human wisdom would take a person who despises the faith and make him into the greatest evangelist of all time![17] From a human perspective, Paul was the least likely person to ever become a follower of Christ, but that is precisely what qualified him for God's service.

At a later point in his life, Paul was unjustly brought to trial before the Roman governors Felix and Festus (Acts 24 and 25). Any human who happened to be at court on those days would have immediately concluded that these rulers had the favor of the gods for they had all the hallmarks of what many assume are signs of God's favor—money, power, and political influence. But contrary to human wisdom, money and power should never be considered signs of God's favor. The truth is that it was Paul, the lowly prisoner, upon whom God's favor rested.

Paul's teaching, like Jesus' teaching, was in complete defiance of human wisdom. He wrote that it was the duty of every Christian to suffer on behalf of the name of Christ (Phil 1:29). He taught that God's power is made perfect not in strength, but in weakness (2 Cor 12:9). He wrote: "Therefore I will boast all the more gladly about my weaknesses, so that Christ's power may rest on me. That is why, for Christ's sake, I delight in weaknesses, in insults, in hardships, in persecutions, in difficulties. For when I am weak, then I am strong" (2 Cor 12:9–10).

The theme of God's defiance of human wisdom is not limited to the contents of the Bible, but is also manifest in its composition. During the Renaissance (AD 1300–1600) there was a renewed interest in classical languages, including the Greek of the New Testament. It was soon recognized that the Greek of the New Testament was peculiar and different from the Greek of classical literature. Some thought that it must be a special form of the Greek language that had been influenced by the Holy Spirit.[18] Eventually it was discovered that the Greek of the New Testament was not a higher form of the Greek language at all, but rather the everyday spoken

---

17. We know that Paul was a real person from history. We have his writings, which contain allusions to his conversion experience that took place that fateful day on the way to Damascus (1 Cor 15:3–8; Gal 1:11–16). There are also three accounts of Paul's conversion experience in the book of Acts (Acts 9:3–9; 22:6–11; 26:12–18). How do we explain such a radical transformation in his life? He claimed that he had seen Jesus somewhere along the way to Damascus. I believe he did too.

18. Dana and Mantey, *Grammar of the New Testament*, 9.

The God Who Defies Human Wisdom

vernacular. Thus, the New Testament writers did not write in an elevated form of the Greek language, but in the vernacular of commoners.[19] This discovery must have been a blow to those who wanted to believe that the Greek of the New Testament was a higher form of the language influenced by the Holy Spirit. But what makes little sense from the perspective of human wisdom makes perfect sense from the perspective of the wisdom of God. God's message is for everyone, not just those trained in the elevated form of classical Greek!

One of the most glaring peculiarities of the New Testament is that much of it is not what we would generally consider great literature, but rather personal letters that the Apostle Paul wrote to specific churches nearly two thousand years ago. Some of his letters contain personal information that have absolutely no personal application for readers today. For example, in 2 Timothy, Paul reminds his traveling companion to bring the cloak that Paul left at Troas, together with certain scrolls and parchments (2 Tim 4:13). Who but the God who defies human wisdom would take personal letters that are conditioned by space and time and use them to speak his timeless message to people throughout all ages! It is highly unlikely that even Paul could have imagined his personal letters would one day be considered scripture alongside the great literature of the Old Testament.

Critics are quick to point out that the Bible is full of contradictions.[20] One of the most glaring discrepancies concerns the death of Judas Iscariot. According to one account, Judas died by hanging (Matt 27:5). According to another account, he died by falling headlong and his body bursting open (Acts 1:18). Of course, it is possible to harmonize these and other contradictory accounts, but admittedly some of the harmonizations seem forced. But there is something intriguing about these contradictions and that is that they remain in the Bible at all when they could have easily been removed by the scribes who transmitted the Bible. The fact that the scribes carefully preserved and passed on the biblical manuscripts the way they did, without ironing out all the discrepancies, demonstrates not only that they really believed that they were transcribing the very oracles of God, but also that the Bible was not manufactured or contrived.[21] "Oh, the depth of

---

19. Dana and Mantey, *Grammar of the New Testament*, 10.

20. Many of these so-called contradictions are only "apparent" and would likely be cleared up with more information.

21. The Hebrew scribes were very careful to preserve and pass on the biblical manuscripts accurately. The Hebrew word for "scribe" means "counter." While we count numbers, the scribes counted letters in order to preserve the accuracy of the biblical

The Ninety-Sixth Thesis

the riches of the wisdom and knowledge of God! How unsearchable his judgments, and his paths beyond tracing out!" (Rom 11:33).

In summary, the God of the Bible reveals himself as a God who defies human wisdom. Sometimes God acts in ways unanticipated by man, while other times he uses the weak to accomplish his will. Either way the point is the same: Nothing is impossible for God! The question now is, how does this insight inform or shape our understanding of God?

It often seems as if Christians have already lost the cultural war. Since Nietzsche, intellectuals have declared God as dead.[22] Moreover, evolution is widely accepted by scientists across the world as a theory that explains the origins of man. In the view of many, this theory contradicts the simple story of creation laid out in book of Genesis. Carroll is certainly correct when he writes that the Reformation, Renaissance, Enlightenment, and science are among the things that have "left traditional religion on the defensive."[23] But what concerns me is that humanity has been set up for a great fall. It would be just like the God of the Bible, a God who acts in defiance of human wisdom, to bait arrogant humans into a trap only to one day show us that we do not know as much as we think we know. An example from academic circles offers a constructive analogy.

Every new academic year professors know that there will be a few new students who will come to class with an excessive amount of over-confidence. Some professors use a technique to check their new students' hubris at the door by baiting them into a trap in order to remind them that they do not know as much as the teacher. Unfortunately, I was baited into one of these traps on the first day of advanced Hebrew in the PhD program at Hebrew Union College. Going into this class, I had every reason to be confident. As a college student, I was recognized as the best Hebrew student in my class. My Hebrew professor was so impressed with my advanced knowledge of the language that he suggested I start learning Arabic, a language closely related to Hebrew. He then began meeting with me privately after Hebrew class to teach me his native Arabic. My Hebrew was so advanced

---

manuscripts. There is a colophon at the end of each book of the Hebrew Bible that gives statistics such as how many sentences, words, and letters are in the book. This information was given to ensure that the next scribe would copy it accurately. Had the scribes not genuinely believed that they were transcribing the very oracles of God, they would not have taken such care to preserve the biblical manuscripts and would have ironed out all the discrepancies.

22. Melchert, *Great Conversation*, 553.
23. Carroll, *Christ Actually*, 33.

The God Who Defies Human Wisdom

that the following semester I was sent across the street to take Hebrew at the seminary with the graduate students. To qualify for this class, I had to pass a graduate-level final exam of a Hebrew class that I had never attended. Not only was I the first one done, but I am sure that I had one of the best grades, if not the best grade, in the entire class!

By the time I entered the PhD program at Hebrew Union College, I already had a master's degree in Hebrew and could read the language exceptionally well. When the professor put a simple sentence on the board and asked for volunteers, naturally I and a few others who were eager to show the professor how well we knew the language raised our hands. Unfortunately, he called on me. With much confidence I read the sentence, but to my surprise the professor said that I read it incorrectly. He asked me if I wanted to try again. I tried two more times and both times he firmly shouted, "Wrong!" Naturally I was a little embarrassed. Although I knew all the words and understood the basic meaning of the sentence, I discovered that the professor got me on a technical matter relating to syntax. But the professor achieved what he set out to accomplish that day and that was to send a message to all the new PhD students that not one of us knew as much about the language as he did. From that point forward, we were much more cautious about raising our hands. But this story contains a valuable lesson for all of us. Humans can be very arrogant, particularly intellectuals, many of whom dismiss even the possibility of the existence of God. But there is a danger in this. Would it not be just like the God of the Bible, a God who defies human wisdom, to bait us arrogant humans into a trap only to one day show us that we do not know as much as we think we know?

The idea of God baiting us arrogant humans into a trap is not merely a suggestion, but is actually forecasted in the Bible. In Matt 11:25, Jesus said the following words: "I praise you, Father, Lord of heaven and earth, *because you have hidden these things from the wise and learned*, and revealed them to little children." Paul writes something very similar to this in the book of 1 Corinthians. In 1 Cor 1:19 God promises to destroy the wisdom of the wise and to frustrate the intelligence of intellectuals. The entire passage is relevant to this discussion.

> For the message of the cross is foolishness to those who are perishing, but to us who are being saved it is the power of God. For it is written: "I will destroy the wisdom of the wise; the intelligence of the intelligent I will frustrate." Where is the wise man? Where is the scholar? Where is the philosopher of this age? Has

> not God made foolish the wisdom of the world? For since in the wisdom of God the world through its wisdom did not know him, God was pleased through the foolishness of what was preached to save those who believe. Jews demand miraculous signs and Greeks look for wisdom, but we preach Christ crucified: a stumbling block to Jews and foolishness to Gentiles, but to those whom God has called, both Jews and Greeks, Christ the power of God and the wisdom of God. For the foolishness of God is wiser than man's wisdom, and the weakness of God is stronger than man's strength. Brothers, think of what you were when you were called. Not many of you were wise by human standards; not many were influential; not many were of noble birth. But God chose the foolish things of the world to shame the wise; God chose the weak things of the world to shame the strong. He chose the lowly things of this world and the despised things—and the things that are not—to nullify the things that are, so that no one may boast before him. (1 Cor 1:18-29)

But what is really concerning about the suggestion that God may be baiting us arrogant humans into a trap is the fact that there are a number of things that make us particularly vulnerable to such a trap.

First, we have a tendency to hear only what we want to hear and to dismiss anything we do not want to hear. Nowhere is this more obvious than in the world of politics. Liberals read the *New York Times* and the *Washington Post* and watch MSNBC and CNN. Conservatives read the *Wall Street Journal* and watch Fox News. Both sides go about their day patting themselves on the back because their worldviews are being confirmed, seemingly unaware that they are seeking out this information from sources who know exactly what their audiences want and expect to hear. There is no such thing as an unbiased interpretation of the facts. Of course, the human desire to hear what we want to hear is nothing new. The kings of the past surrounded themselves with prophets (advisers) who told them exactly what they wanted to hear. History has not been kind to such kings. In the Gospels, Jesus says something peculiar. He says: "He who has ears, let him hear" (Matt 11:15; Luke 14:35, et al.). The point is that although everyone has ears, not everyone listens. The truth is that most of us care less about the truth than confirming what we already believe.

Second, there is a lot of evidence that people are inherently biased and see the world the way they want to see it. One writer asks the question, why do scholars disagree?[24] The short answer is that each scholar has their own *Weltanschauung* or worldview that colors how they see the world. Long writes:

> The individual historian's basic intellectual and spiritual commitments ("how he or she sees the world") exercise an inevitable, even "dominating," influence over which historical reconstructions will appear plausible to that historian. Some historians are theists, others nontheists; some believe in an open universe, others in a closed universe; some regard material forces as the prime motors of historical change, others accord this role to personal (whether human or divine) agency. All of these basic beliefs influence how historians read the biblical texts and at least in part determine whether the Bible's accounts of the past appear plausible or not.[25]

It is important to keep this in mind when assessing the different conclusions reached by scholars. One scholar makes a confession that is highly relevant here: "Thus history is a search for 'what really happened,' but it is also what the historians can convince us really happened."[26] The problem is how to distinguish between "what really happened" and what the historian wants to convince us really happened. Scholars are not unbiased interpreters of facts. There are a lot of factors that have shaped their worldviews. One of these is culture.

Most of us are unaware just how much our beliefs and values are influenced by culture. "Every form of consciousness is a reaction to a way of life that existed before, and an adaption to new realities."[27] For example, the liberalism of the 1960s and 1970s was a reaction to the conservatism of the 1950s. The 1960s and 1970s was a time of rebellion in America. With good reason, Americans had lost faith in authority in general and in the government in particular. The Vietnam War and the failures of the Nixon administration were two of the major catalysts for this. The decades of the 1960s and 1970s produced not only the hippies and the countercultural revolution but also a new way of thinking that rejected the social norms of the 1950s.

---

24. Long, "Art of Biblical History," 358.
25. Long, "Art of Biblical History," 358.
26. Miller, "Reading the Bible Historically," 20.
27. Reich, *Greening of America*, 22.

The Ninety-Sixth Thesis

What were the hippies and the countercultural revolution about? They were anti-reason and anti-authority.[28] The long hair and outlandish clothing of the hippies was an outward expression of their antiauthoritarian spirit. Instead of obedience, they promoted happiness, which included free sex, drugs, and rock-and-roll. Their motto can be summed up in one sentence: do whatever you want, as long as you do not hurt anyone. They promoted the rights of minorities and, to some degree, women.[29] It is reasonable to infer that they opened the door for the gay liberation movement.[30] They were also very concerned about protecting the environment.[31] If all of this sounds familiar it is because the values that were championed by the counterculture of the 1960s and 1970s are the values being promoted in universities across America today. Diversity, inclusion, LGBTQ rights, and climate change are evidence of the enormous impact that the counterculture has had, and continues to have, on America.[32] As the 1950s generation slowly retired and died off, it was only natural that they would be replaced by those who had grown up during the countercultural revolution. The counterculture was the first generation to be college educated in mass. They eventually grew up, cut their hair, put on suits, and took positions of power where they used their platforms to influence how America thinks. I am not trying to pass judgment on the values of the counterculture, but merely trying to show just how much we have been influenced by the liberal values of the counterculture. Why is this relevant to the present discussion? Because it was during these decades that a huge paradigm shift took place in America across many academic fields, a shift away from the conservative views of the 1950s to the much more liberal ones in vogue in universities across America.[33]

---

28. Miller, *Hippies*, 4.

29. Miller, *Hippies*, 15. Miller writes: "Much of the new feminism of the 1970s was spearheaded by women who had logged at least some time among the hippies" (*Hippies*, 137).

30. Miller, *Hippies*, 56–57.

31. Miller, *Hippies*, 133, 137.

32. Some of these changes have made America better place. I personally think that the recognition of the need for diversity is the greatest achievement of the counterculture.

33. This shows that our values and beliefs are in flux and change with culture and are not based on some objective standard. The mistake that we must not make is to assume that our culture's values and beliefs are superior to those of earlier generations. This assumption is particularly tempting when two generations' values are as different as those of the generations of the 1950s and the 1960s/1970s.

The God Who Defies Human Wisdom

The 1950s was a time of respect for authority, especially religious authority. This decade has been called "a high point for the place of religion in the United States."[34] One evidence of this is that there were more churches built at this time than in any other time in American history.[35] In contrast, the 1960s and 1970s was a time of rebellion against authority, including religious authority. "The hippies were enormously hostile to the religious institutions of the dominant culture."[36] This is important to keep in mind when accessing the different conclusions reached by scholars from these very different generations. Working with virtually the same data, scholars from these generations reached polar conclusions regarding the historical reliability of the Bible.

American biblical scholars prior to the 1960s expressed great confidence in the historical reliability of the Bible. W. F. Albright of John's Hopkins University, George Ernest Wright of Harvard, and John Bright of Union Theological Seminary were biblical scholars and archaeologists who believed that the biblical stories were based upon traditions that were rooted in history. In 1942, Albright wrote: "There can be no doubt that archeology has confirmed the substantial historicity of Old Testament tradition."[37] In 1959, Bright took for granted the historical reliability of the Old Testament when he wrote: "The first half of the second millennium B.C. (roughly 2000–1550) brings us to the age of Israel's origins. It was probably during the course of these centuries that Father Abraham set out from Haran, with his family, his flocks, and his herds, to seek land and seed in the place his God would show him."[38] However, the 1970s brought about a new generation of liberal scholars who would swing the pendulum far to the left, in many cases disavowing traditional approaches to the Bible and creating their own models to liberate them from what they perceived as authoritarian interpretations of the Bible.[39] This new generation of scholars would not only not refer to Abraham as father, but would even question

---

34. Hudnut-Beumler, *God in the Suburbs*, 1.
35. Hudnut-Beumler, *God in the Suburbs*, 37.
36. Miller, *Hippies*, 17.
37. Albright, *Archaeology*, 176.
38. John Bright, *History of Israel*, 47.
39. Biblical scholars prior to the 1960s and 1970s were interested in the Bible as history and used what is called the historical-critical method to study the Bible. A number of new models came to light in the 1970s that de-emphasize historical approaches to the Bible and emphasize literary methods of interpretation (see McKenzie and Haynes, *To Each Its Own Meaning*, 6–9).

his very existence.[40] But this raises an important question. Did this new generation of scholars reach their conclusions based upon new evidence or did they merely find what they set out to find? Hoffmeier, an archaeologist and Egyptologist, writes: "Regarding the sojourn and exodus, it is not as though some new compelling archaeological discoveries were made that led to dismissing the history of these crucial (at least to the religion of Israel and OTT) events. Rather it is the consequence of changing views of historiography, that is, the collapse of Enlightenment/scientific methods in the humanities and the rise of postmodern hermeneutics."[41] This 180 degree pendulum swing away from conservative views to much more liberal ones not only in biblical scholarship, but in so many other academic fields all at exactly the same time arouses the suspicion that the sudden change of perspectives had more to do with the *zeitgeist* of the time than with objective analysis of data.[42] The observation that people, including scholars, are inherently biased and often find what they set out to find is just another reason that we are vulnerable to a trap set by the God who promises to defy human wisdom.

Third, we are often taught not how to think but what to think. For example, from the time we are young, we are taught to trust experts.[43] How many television commercials appeal to "experts" to sell their products? These "experts" usually don a white coat and wear glasses and promote products from toothbrushes to medications. The message is clear: you should buy these products because they are endorsed by an expert. Of course, one problem with this is how could anyone know if these "experts" really believe in the products they are promoting or whether they just want to collect a paycheck? But there is an even bigger problem with experts that is more relevant to the present discussion and that is that there are experts

---

40. Kitchen writes: "Here we go back over a generation to the environs of 1970, when a small group of scholars . . . independently reassessed, with negative results, the previous scholarly partial consensus that had favored the possible or probable historicity of the ancestral Hebrew forerunners of earliest Israel (and others besides)" (*Reliability of the Old Testament*, 475).

41. Hoffmeier, "These Things Happened," 104.

42. How else do you explain such a dramatic shift of perspectives over a period of less than thirty years by two generations as ideologically opposed as these ones?

43. There is nothing wrong with seeking expert opinion, but it must always be remembered that experts see things differently and are not unbiased interpreters of facts. It must also always be remembered that evidence is not the same as proof. There are a lot of people who have been unjustly sentenced to prison for life, or even worse, on the basis of evidence.

The God Who Defies Human Wisdom

on every side of every issue. This allows people to make up their minds about an issue first and then find experts to support their already existing beliefs, once again confirming what they already believed!

With all these "experts" one would think that there would be more agreement on the issues. But the truth is, outside of the exact sciences, experts see things very differently. Liberals tend to interpret things one way, while conservatives tend to interpret things another way. The Supreme Court is a perfect example of this. The Supreme Court consists of nine justices who are experts in the law who are supposed to use what they know about the law to make decisions on the most important court cases in America. They are not supposed to allow their personal beliefs or political affiliations influence their decisions. Nevertheless, split decisions are not uncommon on the Supreme Court and it is often the case that the justices vote along party lines in favor of whatever party appointed them to the court! Thus, decisions often seem to be based more on who appointed the justice to the court, rather than on objective analysis of the law.[44] The lack of consistency among experts along with the observation that there are experts on every side of every issue arouses the suspicion that even expert opinion can be extremely subjective.

Fourth, although there are experts on both sides of every issue, the hiring process—particularly at universities—creates the appearance that one side's views are superior to another's by giving one side a platform and silencing the other.[45] It is said that history is written by the winners, but it is also true that worldviews are constructed by those in power. It is natural for people to want others to agree with them and to see the world the way they see it, but the rich and powerful are in a unique position to shape the worldview of others by not only donating large sums of money to champion

---

44. I am sure that justices will emphatically deny that there are conservative and liberal judges, but this is idealistic. Anyone who regularly follows politics knows that some circuits are more liberal than others. Political pundits often refer to the justices of the Supreme Court as liberal and conservative justices. So, while idealistically there should not be conservative or liberal justices, I think we all know better. The very fact that politicians fight over the other sides' appointees to the court betrays an awareness that they have real doubts about any appointee's ability to remain impartial. If politicians truly believed that justices could be impartial, they would not fight so vociferously over the other side's appointees to any court! They could simply draw straws!

45. Just as liberal or conservative justices tend to interpret the law differently, liberal and conservative professors are going to approach the same class very differently. Students, particularly in the humanities, will get an entirely different perspective depending upon the biases and political leanings of their instructors.

certain causes, but also by controlling the hiring process. The hiring process is not an objective process, but rather a subjective process that allows those at the top—particularly at universities—to control the worldview of others. We must constantly resist the temptation of assuming that there is only one side to any issue. Universities are not here to promote the truth, but to promote the truth that is currently demanded by culture.[46] If liberals have taught us anything it is that they love diversity, just not diversity of opinion.

It is well known that college campuses and universities have become bastions of liberalism. Liberals currently have a complete monopoly on both the media and academia.[47] The coming of age of the counterculture is the most logical explanation for this. Are liberals using those powers to make sure that both sides of every issue get a fair hearing? Of course not! University students are getting a one-sided, jaded perspective that champions the values of the liberal left. I am not attacking liberalism. I personally believe that liberals and conservatives mutually benefit society and that it is the respectful dialogue between them that makes a society great. The problem is that many of today's liberals are not interested in respectful dialogue, but in silencing conservatives. In her book *The Silencing: How the Left Is Killing Free Speech*, Powers, a liberal, writes: "The illiberal left doesn't desire debate, it wants a monologue on one side and silence on the other."[48] Earlier in her book, she references two studies that underscore the liberal bias toward conservatives and evangelicals. She references a 2012 study that "found that 82 percent of liberal social psychologists surveyed said they would be at least a little prejudiced against a conservative applicant for a job in their department."[49] "A 2007 study of faculty on college campuses found that 53 percent of university professors had 'cool' or negative feelings towards evangelicals."[50] Powers writes:

---

46. As evidence of this, consider Harvard's original motto, *Veritas Christo et Ecclesiae*, "Truth for Christ and Church," later changed to *Veritas*, "Truth." Culture changed and the university changed to accommodate it!

47. Powers, a liberal, freely admits: "Conservatives simply do not control the primary institutions where free speech is most under assault: the media and academia" (*Silencing*, 9).

48. Powers, *Silencing*, 33.

49. José L. Duarte et al., "Political Diversity Will Improve Social Psychological Science," *Behavioral and Brain Sciences* (Cambridge University Press, 2014), https://journals.cambridge.org/images/fileUpload/documents/Duarte-Haidt_BBS-D-14-0108_preprint.pdf, cited in Powers, *Silencing*, xiii.

50. Gary A. Tobin and Aryeh K. Weinberg, "Profiles of the American University: Volume II: Religious Beliefs & Behavior of College Faculty," Institute for Jewish & Community Research, 2007, http://www.jewishresearch.org/PDFs2/FacultyReligion07.pdf,

"This raises serious questions about how Christian students can expect to be treated on secular campuses."[51] But it goes further than this because studies like these demonstrate just how easy it is for those in power to control worldviews. If colleges or universities do not like conservatives or a particular group's worldview, they simply do not have to hire them!

Fifth, because liberals have a complete stranglehold on both the media and academia, they are in danger of a groupthink phenomenon where powerful people surround themselves with like-minded individuals and then talk themselves into whatever it is they want to believe. If someone dissents, they are simply removed from the group. When Robert McNamara alone among the president's advisors opposed the Johnson administration's Vietnam War policy, he was eventually removed from his position of secretary of defense.[52] "Once McNamara was removed from the group . . . the members could once again enjoy complete unity and relatively undisturbed confidence in the soundness of their war policy."[53] As we all know now, the results of that decision were catastrophic. Whether wittingly or unwittingly, the media and academia exercise this same control when they hire only other liberals.[54] Unfortunately, group think manifests itself in other ways in the academy.

For the past one hundred years, biblical scholarship has been dominated by a theory called the documentary hypothesis, which proposed that the Pentateuch, the first five books of the Bible, was not written by Moses as tradition says, but was the product of the compilation of four independent sources (J,E, D, and P) from four different periods of time that were eventually woven together into one story.[55] So confident were scholars of the

---

cited in Powers, *Silencing*, xiii.

51. Powers, *Silencing*, xiii.

52. Janis, *Groupthink*, 117–20.

53. Janis, *Groupthink*, 119.

54. We all could learn a lot from business tycoon Lee Iacocca, who writes that one of the most important lessons that he learned in business was the value of different perspectives. He writes: "If all you're getting from your team is a single point of view—usually *your* point of view—you've got to worry. You can get your own point of view for *free*" (*Where Have All the Leaders Gone?*, 19).

55. Whybray, *Making of the Pentateuch*, 17. The letter J derives from the Hebrew personal name of God *Yhwh* (in German, *Jhwh*) and represents the Yahwistic source, E derives from the Hebrew name for God *Elohim*. The letter D represents the Deuteronomistic source and P represents the priestly source. Scholars believed that the different names for God in the Bible were an indication of multiple authorship. It is hard to believe that a theory based upon such a simplistic observation could ever gain any traction, but it did. Whybray has suggested that the choice of one divine name over another might

assured results of this theory that anyone who did not accept its basic tenets was immediately dismissed as someone with a conservative ax to grind. Its near universal acceptance in the academy can only be compared with theories that are widely accepted throughout the academic world, such as the theory of evolution. There were of course a few scholars who expressed doubts about this theory from the beginning, but they were largely ignored because scholars were caught up in the enthusiasm of their creativity. However, despite all the confidence of earlier scholars, the entire theory is now in serious doubt and the criticism is no longer coming from conservative biblical scholars, but from mainline biblical scholars who cannot be accused of having a conservative ax to grind. Whybray, one of these mainline scholars, writes: "There is at the present moment no consensus whatever about when, why, how, and through whom the Pentateuch reached its present form, and opinions about the dates of composition of its various parts differ by more than five hundred years."[56] Whybray writes: "The variety of conclusions which have been reached by scholars from the time of Wellhausen onwards . . . arouses the suspicion that the methods employed are extremely subjective."[57] The question that must be asked is, how could a theory dominate an academic field for so long and be widely accepted by so many scholars and then suddenly fall out of favor? Scholars, like people in general, are very good at talking themselves into whatever it is that they want to believe and getting others to buy in. What most people do not realize is that scholars do a lot of guessing. We must never mistake confidence

---

have been an unconscious decision, much like people today use different titles to refer to God. Some call him Lord, others call him the Almighty, etc. "Such unconscious variations in the choice of words occur frequently in ordinary speech, and also in modern books" (*Making of the Pentateuch*, 72). Cassuto and Segal have shown that the choice of one divine name over another was often done for theological and stylistic reasons (*Making of the Pentateuch*, 72). "The reliability of the criteria was also unwittingly put in doubt by those critics who used them to postulate, by an even more minute analysis, the existence of yet more documents, so demonstrating that the same methods could produce quite different results" (Whybray, *Making of the Pentateuch*, 29). Allow me to be candid here and make a confession. It was not until I became a scholar and had the ability to evaluate the work of my peers and to see firsthand what was made out of the flimsiest of arguments in favor of the documentary hypothesis that I realized that scholars can talk themselves into anything. As Whybray has noted, in many cases "conjecture has been piled upon conjecture" (Whybray, *Making of the Pentateuch*, 15). If scholars are capable of this in biblical scholarship, why should I uncritically accept the results of scholars from any other academic field?

56. Whybray, *Introduction to the Pentateuch*, 12–13.
57. Whybray, *Making of the Pentateuch*, 233.

for truth. There are a lot of people who have been 100 percent confident about something only to find out later they were 100 percent wrong! Consensus means very little when people are simply talking themselves into whatever it is that they want to believe.

Finally, the rise of postmodern hermeneutics is perhaps what makes us most vulnerable to a trap set by the God who defies wisdom. Broadly speaking, modernism describes the period of time from approximately the Enlightenment (the beginning of the 18th century) through the 1950s when people generally believed in objective truth and that truth could be found through reason. Postmodernism, on the other hand, describes the period of time from the 1960s until now when people reject modernism's belief in absolute truth. Although the counterculture did not create postmodernism, they eagerly embraced it because of its antiauthoritarian spirit. Postmodernism says that there is no objective truth and that truth is relative to the individual. "Your truth is your truth, but my truth is my truth," so the saying goes. This shift toward postmodernism has led to an entirely new way of reading texts, including religious texts such as the Bible. In the modern period, people read to discover the author's meaning. In the postmodern period, the reader is not interested in the author's meaning, but in what the text means to the reader. In other words, it is the reader who determines the meaning of any text, including religious texts such as the Bible![58] But this creates a dilemma for God, who has chosen to communicate to humanity through the Bible. Vanhoozer writes: "From a Christian perspective, God is first and foremost a communicative agent, one who relates to humankind through words and the Word."[59] If words are stripped of their meaning, then the Bible and other religious books are stripped of all authority and their ability to convey meaning. "If meaning is not there, then there is nothing to be known and nothing for which interpreters are responsible. As a result, the author is pronounced 'dead' on the reader's arrival. The death of the author 'thus liberates an activity we may call counter-theological . . . for to refuse to halt meaning is finally to refuse God.'"[60] Thus, postmodern hermeneutics is the ultimate form of rebellion because it is an attack not only on authority in general, but on God and the Bible in particular. The

---

58. The shift of thinking with regard to the way people now read texts is nicely captured in the title of a book on biblical interpretation: "To Each Its Own Meaning" (McKenzie and Haynes, *To Each Its Own Meaning*).

59. Vanhoozer, *Is There a Meaning in This Text*, 456.

60. Vanhoozer, *Is There a Meaning in This Text*, 457. In the last sentence, Vanhoozer quotes Barthes, "Death of the Author," 54.

The Ninety-Sixth Thesis

message from humanity to God could not be any clearer: We do not care about truth, but in seeing the world the way we want to see it!

We have all met people who get angry when we do not agree with them. Metaphorically they kick tables and throw chairs. Imagine what such people would do if they only had a little power! Powerful people are trying to shape our worldviews. They are the ones who hire the scholars who wield the pen to do their bidding.[61] But we must constantly resist the temptation of assuming that there is only one side to any issue. There are other perspectives but unfortunately they are all too often denied platforms, particularly at universities that pander to the liberal left for fear of losing both state and federal funding.[62] If this chapter accomplishes anything, I hope it draws attention to the need for diversity of perspectives in academia.[63] Just like we demand diversity of race, gender, and ethnicity, we must start demanding diversity of perspectives that includes both liberals and conservatives if for no other reason than that we do not end up talking ourselves into that

---

61. Most of us are unaware of the enormous influence and control that money wields over us. How do powerful countries get rogue nations to do what they want them to do without going to war? They place economic sanctions on them until they comply. Employers do this too. As the political winds have shifted further to the left, we have seen both companies and universities become more vocal in their support of liberal causes. Powerful people are using both their money and platforms to influence how we think. They are not interested in authenticity, but in complete conformity. Those who hold the purse strings are, in at least some cases, literally forcing their employees to accept liberal values or at the very least to pay lip service to them. Never before has there been more pressure to conform.

62. I am reminded of Paul's words: "The love of money is the root of all evil" (1 Tim 6:10). Just the threat that students could lose access to federal funding or FAFSA is enough to make universities toe the line. They do not fear conservatives who want to conserve society, but liberals who want to alter it and will use any power available to achieve that end. Consider, for example, the Obama administration's threat to withhold funding from those institutions that oppose Title IX. Title IX was originally intended to end institutional limitations on opportunities for women, but today it is used much more broadly to regulate other, more controversial, issues that are championed by liberals. When powerful people threaten to withhold funding, is it really so amazing when institutions simply choose to get on board?

63. I could not agree more with Powers, who concludes: "Liberals are supposed to believe in diversity, which should include diversity of thought and belief. Instead, an alarming level of intolerance emanates from the left side of the political spectrum toward people who express views that don't hew to the 'settled' liberal worldview. The passion for silencing isn't reserved for conservatives or orthodox Christians. Moderate Democrats, independent minded liberals, and the ideologically agnostic become targets if they deviate on liberal sacred cow issues" (*Silencing*, xiii–xiv).

The God Who Defies Human Wisdom

which we want to believe.[64] Outside of the exact sciences, conclusions are not as clear-cut as many scholars would like us to believe. Whybray offers a warning about the self-assurance of scholars with regard to the formulation of the Pentateuch that should apply to the conclusions reached in any academic field.

> It is therefore difficult to avoid the conclusion that the likelihood of modern scholars' succeeding in discovering—except, perhaps, in very general terms—how the Pentateuch was compiled is small indeed. This does not necessarily mean that it is not worthwhile to make the attempt. But the self-assurance with which many scholars, especially during the past hundred years, have propounded their views on the subject should be regarded with suspicion. Every hypothesis which has been advanced needs to be carefully scrutinized with respect both to its method and to its hidden presuppositions and assumptions. It will be found that often conjecture has been piled upon conjecture.[65]

These observations—that we hear what we want to hear, that we often find what we set out to find, that we are often taught not how to think but what to think, that we have a tendency to hire only those who agree with us, the arrival of postmodern hermeneutics, etc.,—make us particularly vulnerable to a trap set by the God who promises to defy human wisdom. Humans in their hubris are being baited into a trap and it is the God who promises to defy human wisdom who has set the bait.

Rudolf Bultmann, considered by many as one of the great theological minds of the twentieth century, wrote: "It is impossible to use electric light and the wireless and to avail ourselves of modern medical and surgical discoveries, and at the same time to believe in the New Testament world of spirits and miracles."[66] The problem is that may be exactly what the God who promises to defy human wisdom wants humans to think.

---

64. Humans can talk themselves into anything, especially if they benefit from it in some way.
65. Whybray, *Making of the Pentateuch*, 15.
66. Bultmann, "New Testament and Mythology," 5.

Chapter 5

The Story of Abraham

There may be some reading this who are more interested in the Bible now and would like to learn more about it but do not know where to start. I want to conclude this book with the Old Testament story of Abraham that I introduced in the preceding chapter. There are two reasons for this. First, it sets the stage for what the Bible is all about. Second, it offers one of the most compelling reasons to believe that the Bible is indeed the word of God and that Jesus is the Christ.

Before delving into this subject, a clarification is necessary. The claim that the Bible is the word of God requires an explanation. To some this means one thing, to others this means something else. The important thing is to be open-minded here because we are addressing a subject that is debated even among Christians. Some Christians believe that the entire Bible from Genesis to Revelation is literally true and that everything happened exactly as the Bible records. Other Christians take a more liberal approach and believe in the historicity of major events such as the resurrection of Christ, but not necessarily in the historicity of every minor detail of every biblical story. I have my beliefs about this, but I think it is important for readers to reach their own conclusions about such things.[1] Although I will not explain all my beliefs, I will say that I believe that Abram and Sarai and the other people we read about in the Bible were

---

[1] I genuinely believe that there is room for different perspectives. One reason for this is that God has not made things entirely clear. I can only conclude that he must not want things to be entirely clear. It is for this reason that I rarely tell my students exactly what I believe. I do not want them to think like me; I want them to think for themselves and to reach their own conclusions.

real people whose encounters with God are accurately and faithfully recorded in the Bible.[2]

In the preceding chapter we learned that God created the world to be a good place (Gen 1–2). According to the Genesis account, there was no sin, death, or evil. The world was created to be a true utopia where humans were to live forever and enjoy fellowship with God. But something went tragically wrong. The first man and woman disobeyed God and brought a terrible curse upon the world that resulted in widespread sin and death (Gen 3). But, as we learned in the preceding chapter, sin and death were only part of the problem. The real problem from the biblical perspective was that the fellowship shared by God and man was now broken. No longer would God walk with man in the garden in the cool of the day (Gen 3:8). Instead, man would be driven out from the garden and away from God's presence.

It is no coincidence that immediately after the story of man's disobedience in the garden of Eden, the Bible records a number of tragic stories in rapid succession (Gen 4–11). These stories were summarized in the preceding chapter. The placement of these stories immediately after the fall is no coincidence, but the writer's way of driving home the point that the world is spiraling out of control as a result of the curse. At the end of this unit (Gen 4–11), the reader is left only to wonder if there is any way to reverse the curse that had befallen mankind? Is there any way to reconcile God and man? It is at this point of the book of Genesis that the Bible introduces Abram, the man who is God's solution to the curse.

In Gen 12:1–3, God revealed himself to Abram and made several significant promises to him.

> The LORD had said to Abram, "Leave your country, your people and your father's household and go to the land I will show you. I will make you into a great nation and I will bless you; I will make your name great, and you will be a blessing. I will bless those who bless you, and whoever curses you I will curse; and all peoples on earth will be blessed through you."

---

2. There are good reasons to believe that the personalities we read about in the Bible were historical. Many of the names of important figures from the Bible, including Pontius Pilate and John the Baptist, are known from extrabiblical sources. Even the names of obscure Old Testament personalities, such as Mesha the king of Moab (2 Kgs 3:4), have been found in extrabiblical sources. For those interested in this subject, I highly recommend K. A. Kitchen's book *On the Reliability of the Old Testament*.

The Ninety-Sixth Thesis

The Bible does not explain how God spoke to Abram. All it says is that God told Abram to leave his family and his country to go to a new land that God would show him. God then promised to bless Abram in several significant ways. First, God promised to make Abram into a great nation. Second, God promised to *bless* him. Third, God promised to make Abram's name great so that he would be a *blessing*. Fourth, God promised that Abram and his seed would be a *blessing* to others. Fifth, God promised to *bless* those who *bless* Abram. Sixth, God promised to curse those who curse Abram. Seventh, and most importantly, God promised that all people on earth would somehow be *blessed* through Abram.

As we learned in the preceding chapter, the word "blessing" occurs repeatedly in this passage and is obviously significant. The repetition of this word is a literary cue that God indeed has a plan to reverse the curse and this plan has something to do with Abram. This is indicated not only by the repetition of the word "blessing" but also by the climactic promise that comes at the end (v. 3), which states that *all people on earth will be blessed through Abram*. Wright explains: "Now the main point of God's promise to Abram was not merely that he would have a son, and thereby descendants who would be especially blessed by God, but that through that people of Abram God would bring blessing to *all nations* of the earth."[3]

Abram was seventy-five years old and his wife was sixty-five at the time of these promises (Gen 12:4; 17:17). Thus, God's promises to Abram were entirely contingent upon the unrealistic possibility of a sixty-five-year-old woman giving birth. Of course, human wisdom would immediately conclude that such is impossible; sixty-five-year-old women cannot give birth![4] However, as we learned in the preceding chapter, that is exactly what the God who defies human wisdom wants humans to think. It is at this point that we pick up our story. Something very significant happens in it that everyone should be made aware of.

After several years had passed, God came to Abram in a vision and reiterated the promise that he and Sarai would have a child in their old age.

> After this, the word of the LORD came to Abram in a vision: "Do not be afraid, Abram. I am your shield, your very great reward."
> But Abram said, "O Sovereign LORD, what can you give me since

---

3. Wright, *Knowing Jesus*, 4.

4. Although not common, women over the age of fifty have given birth after getting pregnant naturally. A number of news outlets have reported a story about a Chinese woman who gave birth at the age of sixty-seven after getting pregnant naturally!

The Story of Abraham

> I remain childless and the one who will inherit my estate is Eliezer of Damascus?" And Abram said, "You have given me no children; so a servant in my household will be my heir." Then the word of the LORD came to him: "This man will not be your heir, but a son coming from your own body will be your heir." He took him outside and said, "Look up at the heavens and count the stars—if indeed you can count them." Then he said to him, "So shall your offspring be." Abram believed the LORD, and he credited it to him as righteousness. (Gen 15:1–6)

What is different in this passage from Gen 12:1–3 is that God does not just promise that Abram and Sarai will have a child in their old age, but swears to it with an oath. That is the point of the ritual that follows (Gen 15:7–21). Cutting animals into halves sounds terribly cruel according to modern standards, but this was a well-known covenant ritual in the ancient Near East. In English the expression is to "make" a covenant, but in Hebrew the expression is always to "cut" a covenant. After the animals were cut into halves, the two agreeing parties would walk through the path of blood between the animal halves signifying that both parties intended to keep the stipulations of the covenant lest the curse of becoming like the divided animals befall them.[5] But in this instance Abram had fallen into a deep sleep, no doubt put upon him by God, and God alone walked down the path signifying that God's promises to Abram were not dependent upon Abram, but upon God and the faithfulness of his guaranteed oath.

However, it is at this point in the narrative that tension begins to build, because God is going to allow more years to pass before fulfilling his promise. During these years of waiting, even Abram and Sarai began to entertain doubts about God's ability to bring his promise to fruition (Gen 16:1–2; 17:17–18; 18:11–12).

It is important to remember what is at stake here. Any delay is a threat not only to the birth of this child, but also to the very promises that God made to Abram. If this child is not born, then not only can God not make Abram into a great nation, but he cannot fulfill his promise to bless all people on earth through Abram and his descendants.

When Abram was eighty-five years old and Sarai was seventy-five, Sarai decided that it was time to take action and help God fulfill his promise.

> Now Sarai, Abram's wife, had borne him no children. But she had an Egyptian maidservant named Hagar; so she said to Abram,

---

5. Anderson, *Understanding the Old Testament*, 44.

The Ninety-Sixth Thesis

> "The LORD has kept me from having children. Go, sleep with my maidservant; perhaps I can build a family through her." Abram agreed to what Sarai said. So after Abram had been living in Canaan ten years, Sarai his wife took her Egyptian maidservant Hagar and gave her to her husband to be his wife. (Gen 16:1–3)

Sarai's idea worked exactly as planned. Abram slept with Hagar and she conceived and gave birth to a son, Ishmael (Gen 16:4, 15). Ishmael is recognized today as the father of the Arab peoples. Abram loved Ishmael and wanted him to be the child of the promise (Gen 17:18). God loved Ishmael too and promised to bless him also, but was he the child that God had promised Abram and Sarai? God's oath promised that Abram and Sarai would have a son that would come from their own bodies (Gen 15:4). In order to remind Abram and Sarai of that promise, God changed their names. God changed Abram's name to Abraham (Gen 17:5) and Sarai's name to Sarah (Gen 17:15). While Abram means "exalted father," Abraham means "father of many."[6] The change of name indicated that Abraham would indeed become the father of many people and this people would become a "great nation" (Gen 12:2), the nation of Israel.

> God also said to Abraham, "As for Sarai your wife, you are no longer to call her Sarai; her name will be Sarah. I will bless her and will surely give you a son by her. I will bless her so that she will be the mother of nations; kings of peoples will come from her." Abraham fell facedown; he laughed and said to himself, "Will a son be born to a man a hundred years old? Will Sarah bear a child at the age of ninety?" And Abraham said to God, "If only Ishmael might live under your blessing!" Then God said, "Yes, but your wife Sarah will bear you a son, and you will call him Isaac. I will establish my covenant with him as an everlasting covenant for his descendants after him." (Gen 17:15–19)

Abram was eighty-six years old and Sarai was seventy-six when Hagar bore Ishmael (Gen 16:16). However, God was not done acting in defiance of human wisdom. God would allow thirteen more years to pass before finally fulfilling his promise.

At the end of those thirteen years, Abraham was visited by three messengers who arrived with an important message (Gen 18).[7] They an-

---

6. Sarai and Sarah are different pronunciations of a word that means "princess" (Wenham, *Genesis 16–50*, 25).

7. Anytime angels appear in the Bible they always come with an important message. They are often disguised as humans, which explains why Abraham thought they were

The Story of Abraham

nounced to Abraham that the time had come for God to fulfill his promise. According to these three visitors, Sarah would give birth the following year. Gen 18:9–14 reads:

> "Where is your wife Sarah?" they asked him. "There, in the tent," he said. Then the LORD said, "I will surely return to you about this time next year, and Sarah your wife will have a son." Now Sarah was listening at the entrance to the tent, which was behind him. Abraham and Sarah were already old and well advanced in years, and Sarah was past the age of childbearing. So Sarah laughed to herself as she thought, "After I am worn out and my master is old, will I now have this pleasure?" Then the LORD said to Abraham, "Why did Sarah laugh and say, 'Will I really have a child, now that I am old?' Is anything too hard for the LORD? I will return to you at the appointed time next year and Sarah will have a son."

The next year, when Abraham was one hundred years old and Sarah was ninety (Gen 21:5), the Lord finally fulfilled the promise that he had made to Abraham twenty-five years earlier. Sarah gave birth to a son and Abraham named him Isaac which means "laughter" (Gen 21:1–5). "Sarah said, 'God has brought me laughter, and everyone who hears about this will laugh with me.' And she added, 'Who would have said to Abraham that Sarah would nurse children? Yet I have borne him a son in his old age'" (Gen 21:6–7).

How happy Abraham and Sarah must have been! Not only had God finally fulfilled his promise and gave the old couple a child, but all the promises that were contingent upon the birth of this child were no longer in doubt. The promise to reverse the curse and to bless all people of the world through Abram and his descendants could now come to fruition (Gen 12:3). But it is at this point of the narrative that the story takes a surprising and unexpected twist when God tells Abraham to take his only son Isaac, the one whom he loves, and sacrifice him on one of the mountains God would show him (Gen 22:1–2)!

The Old Testament is very clear with regard to the sanctity of life. Murder is forbidden not only in the Ten Commandments (Exod 20:13), but also in one of the earliest chapters of the book of Genesis (Gen 9:6). The main reason for the prohibition against murder is that man is created in the image of God (Gen 9:6). These clear prohibitions against murder

---

men (Gen 18). It is for this reason that the book of Hebrews admonishes us to entertain strangers for some have entertained angels unwittingly (Heb 13:2).

The Ninety-Sixth Thesis

make God's command to Abraham all the more peculiar. Why is God asking Abraham to do something that God has forbidden elsewhere? This is one of only a handful of passages in the Bible where God asks someone to deliberately violate one of his commandments.[8] This is the Bible's way of cueing the reader to pay attention because something very significant is about to happen.

Gen 22:1-2 reads:

> Sometime later God tested Abraham. He said to him, "Abraham!" "Here I am," he replied. Then God said, "Take your son, your only son, Isaac, whom you love, and go to the region of Moriah. Sacrifice him there as a burnt offering on one of the mountains I will tell you about."

The narrative begins by letting the reader know an important detail that Abraham was unaware of: God was only testing Abraham; God never intended for Abraham to sacrifice his son. Abraham learns this only later when an Angel of God stops him from sacrificing Isaac (Gen 22:11–12). But this raises an important question that will have to be answered later. Why would God ask Abraham to sacrifice his son if God never intended for him to do it?

It is important to note that the promises that God made to Abraham twenty-five years earlier are, once again, under threat. If Abraham sacrifices Isaac, not only can God not make Abraham into a great nation and give him descendants as numerous as the stars in the sky, but he cannot fulfill his promise to reverse the curse by blessing all people on earth through him and his descendants (seed). It almost seems as if God is taunting humans to disbelieve him. He seems to relish in apparent threats to his promises.

In addition to God's unexpected command to sacrifice Isaac, there are other elements of surprise in this story that are worthy of attention. One of these is the peculiar reference to Isaac as Abraham's "only" son (Gen 22:2). Why is Isaac called the "only" son when in fact readers have already been informed that Abraham has another son named Ishmael, whom Hagar bore at the behest of Sarai? Details such as this are rarely incidental.

To the astonishment of the reader, it becomes clear that Abraham fully intends to obey God and sacrifice his "only" son!

---

8. God told Hosea to marry a harlot as a symbol of Israel's unfaithfulness to God (Hos 1:1–2).

The Story of Abraham

> Early the next morning Abraham got up and saddled his donkey. He took with him two of his servants and his son Isaac. When he had cut enough wood for the burnt offering, he set out for the place God had told him about. On the third day Abraham looked up and saw the place in the distance. He said to his servants, "Stay here with the donkey while I and the boy go over there. We will worship and then we will come back to you." (Gen 22:3–5)

As they climbed up the mountain, Isaac, seemingly unaware of what was about to happen, asked his father: "The fire and wood are here . . . but where is the lamb for the burnt offering?" Abraham answered, "God himself will provide the lamb for the burnt offering, my son." And the two of them went on together (Gen 22:7–8).

Finally, they reached the place where God told Abraham to go. Abraham built an altar and laid his beloved son upon it. There could no longer be any doubt in Isaac's mind regarding his father's intentions.

> When they reached the place God had told him about, Abraham built an altar there and arranged the wood on it. He bound his son Isaac and laid him on the altar, on top of the wood. Then he reached out his hand and took the knife to slay his son. (Gen 22:9–10)

It is at this point of the narrative that the story takes another bizarre twist. As Abraham raised his hand to slay his son, God's angel suddenly appeared and abruptly stopped Abraham from sacrificing his son.

> But the angel of the LORD called out to him from heaven, "Abraham! Abraham!" "Here I am," he replied. "Do not lay a hand on the boy," he said. "Do not do anything to him. Now I know that you fear God, because you have not withheld from me your son, your only son." (Gen 22:11–12)

What is going on in this chapter? Clearly God was testing Abraham to see if he indeed feared God (Gen 22:12),[9] but one gets the impression that there is more to this story. This conclusion is reinforced by the prophecy that concludes the narrative which states that something significant will take place on this mountain in the distant future.

> So Abraham called that place The LORD Will Provide. And to this day it is said, "On the mountain of the LORD it will be provided." (Gen 22:14)

---

9. The expression "God fearer" is the Old Testament equivalent of "believer."

The Ninety-Sixth Thesis

There are two questions that must be asked here. First, what is it that will be provided on this mountain in the future?[10] Second, why did God test Abraham by asking him to sacrifice his "only" son when God never intended for Abraham to follow through with it?

The place where the story of Abraham's sacrifice of Isaac takes place is identified as Moriah (Gen 22:2). Mt. Moriah is mentioned only one other time in the Old Testament. Years later, king David would buy a threshing floor here from a person named Araunah the Jebusite. David would purchase this threshing floor and build an altar upon it because it was on this very spot that the Lord relented from destroying the people of Israel with a terrible plague which was brought upon them by the sin of David (2 Sam 24; 1 Chr 21). The significance of this purchase comes to light only later when David's son Solomon builds the temple of God upon it (2 Chr 3:1). Thus, the mountain where God told Abraham to sacrifice Isaac turns out to be the place where Solomon's temple will eventually be built hundreds of years later. One can easily make the case then, as Jews naturally do, that the prophecy that concludes the narrative must refer to the building of Solomon's temple in Jerusalem.

Years earlier, God promised Abraham that all people on earth would be blessed through him and his descendants (Gen 12:1–3), but God did not explain how. Now we can make some sense of this. Solomon is going to build the temple of God on the mountain where Abraham intended to sacrifice Isaac. This temple would become a blessing to all people because in it God and man would be reconciled via the sacrificial system.[11] The temple would eventually become the place where the fellowship God and

---

10. A literal translation of the Hebrew is: "It/he will be seen" or "It/he will appear." Hamilton writes that any of the following translations are possible: "In the mountain of Yahweh he is seen," "In the mountain of Yahweh he shall be seen," or "In the mountain of Yahweh it shall be provided" (*Genesis*, 114).

11. The sacrificial system sounds terribly cruel today, but there was a reason for it. Permit me to offer a simplified explanation of it. According to the Bible, all men are sinners and because of that deserve death. Just as a judge cannot allow someone who is guilty to go unpunished, a holy God cannot allow sins to go unpunished. Justice demands that the guilty be punished. Through the sacrificial system God allowed an animal to die in place of the sinner. The sinner would lay hands on the animal, thus transferring his sins to the innocent animal, and watch as the priest slit its throat. This act was intended to remind the sinner of the seriousness of his sin. For Christians these sacrifices are no longer necessary because they pointed forward to the time in the future when God would offer his only son Jesus for the sins of the world.

The Story of Abraham

man once shared would be restored. It would be the place where God and man would walk together in harmony as they once did in Eden.[12]

It is important to remember that God promised that all people on earth—not just Jews—would be blessed through Abram and his descendants. This also fits our interpretation of this passage in that the temple of Solomon would benefit not just Jews, but also Gentiles. Anyone who feared God was permitted to worship in this temple.[13] It is well known that the Jews are God's chosen people. But what most people do not know is the reason they were chosen. According to the book of Exodus, the Jews were chosen to be a kingdom of priests whose role was to teach the rest of the world about the one true God (Exod 19:6). The temple is the place where this would happen. Thus, there can be no doubt that Solomon's temple was a blessing to all people, including both Jews and Gentiles.

It would appear then that the Jewish temple that once stood in Jerusalem is the fulfillment of God's promise to bless all people on earth through Abraham and his descendants. Not only does this interpretation make sense in light of the promises God made to Abraham, but it also seems to fulfill the prophecy of Gen 22:14 that concludes the narrative and states that, in the future, something else will be provided on this mountain. But is the temple of Solomon all that is alluded to in these passages, or is there perhaps an allusion to something more profound?

There can be no doubt that the story of Abraham's sacrifice of Isaac had been written long before the time of Jesus. H. G. Wells writes: "All the books that constitute the Old Testament were certainly in existence, and in

---

12. It is no coincidence that the temple shares remarkable similarities with the garden of Eden. Gordon Wenham is to be credited with this discovery. He notes that there are two places in the Bible where God is said to have "walked," one of these is the garden of Eden and the other is the tabernacle (Gen 3:8; Lev 26:12; Deut 23:15; 2 Sam 7:6–7). Second, the garden of Eden, the tabernacle, and the temple were all entered from the east and cherubs or angels guarded the way to Eden and the later sanctuaries. Third, the tree of life is also a sanctuary symbol. "Trees were sometimes planted by the patriarchs at places where they worshipped (Gen 21:33), and were a regular feature of Canaanite and later shrines." There is also evidence that the menorah itself is a symbol of the tree of life. Fourth, the Bible says that God put Adam in the garden "to work it and take care of it." The Hebrew verbs "to work and take care of" are used in combination elsewhere in the Pentateuch only to describe the activities of the Levites in the sanctuary (Num 3:7–8; 8:26; 18:5–6). Finally, gold and precious gems decorated both the garden of Eden and the later sanctuaries. These parallels suggest to Wenham that the garden of Eden was perceived as a sanctuary, a place where man would worship God (Wenham, "Symbolism in the Garden of Eden," 19–24). See also Alexander, *Paradise to the Promised Land*, 131.

13. 1 Kgs 8:41–43; Isa 56:7.

The Ninety-Sixth Thesis

very much their present form, at latest by the year 100 B.C. Most of them were probably recognized as sacred writings in the time of Alexander the Great (330 B.C.)."[14] How do we know this? First, the Hebrew scriptures (the Old Testament) had already been translated into Greek approximately two hundred years before Jesus' birth. Obviously, the Old Testament had to have already been written before it could have been translated into another language. Second, the Dead Sea Scrolls were discovered in 1947. These are the oldest biblical manuscripts ever discovered. Some of these manuscripts predate the time of Christ by more than two hundred years.[15] Why is this so significant? Because here in the Old Testament, hundreds of years before Jesus was born, is a story remarkably and even eerily similar to the New Testament story, a story about another father (God) who would one day sacrifice his "only" son (Jesus) for the sins of the world.

While Christians would agree that the temple was a fulfillment of the promise to bless all people through Abram (Gen 12:3), we believe that there is more to this story. The temple itself does not adequately explain the peculiar details of Genesis 22 such as why God very specifically asked Abraham to sacrifice his son and why God referred to Isaac as Abraham's "only" son when in fact Abraham had another son. The Christian explanation makes sense of all this. The reason God asked Abraham to sacrifice his "only" son is because that is what God always intended to do with his "only" son when he would one day sacrifice Jesus for the sins of the world. Several clues in this story reinforce this interpretation.

First, there is the peculiar emphasis on Isaac being Abraham's "only" son (Gen 22:2), when in fact Abraham had another son. Why would God refer to Isaac as Abraham's only son when in fact Abraham had another son named Ishmael? Details such as this are rarely incidental. Is it merely a coincidence that the New Testament calls Jesus Christ God's "only" son? John 3:16 reads: "For God so loved the world that he gave his one and *only* Son, that whoever believes in him shall not perish but have eternal life."[16]

---

14. Wells, *Outline of History*, 204.

15. Cross writes: "The biblical scrolls from Qumrân span in date about three centuries. A few archaic specimens carry us back to the end of the third century, as we have seen. The heavy majority, however, date in the first century B.C. and in the first Christian century, the series terminating with the death of the community center in A.D. 68" (*Library of Qumran*, 43).

16. The New JPS translation (a Jewish translation) translates "only son" (Gen 22:2) as "favored one." This is an obvious attempt to downplay what looks like an obvious Christian overtone.

The Story of Abraham

Second, Abraham's sacrifice of Isaac is not to take place just anywhere, but at a very specific place called Moriah. As we have learned, Mt. Moriah was the place where Solomon's temple would eventually be built. But was it also the place where Jesus was crucified? Although the precise location of Jesus' crucifixion is still debated, there can be no doubt that it took place somewhere in the region of Moriah. According to the New Testament, Jesus was crucified just outside the city of Jerusalem at a place called Golgotha.[17]

Third, the narrative concludes with a prophecy that promises that something significant will be provided on this mountain in the future. Abraham called this place "The LORD Will Provide" (Gen 22:14). But what is it that will be provided? A clue is found in Abraham's response to Isaac when he asked his father where the lamb was for the burnt offering (Gen 22:7). Abraham responded by saying that God would provide *the lamb* for the burnt offering (Gen 22:8). Is it merely a coincidence that the New Testament calls Jesus "the lamb of God, who takes away the sin of the world" (John 1:29).

Finally, the narrative concludes by tying this prophecy to the earlier promise to bless all people on earth through Abraham and his descendants (Gen 12:3).

> The angel of the LORD called to Abraham from heaven a second time and said, "I swear by myself, declares the LORD, that because you have done this and have not withheld your son, your only son,

---

17. The fact that God told Abraham to sacrifice Isaac on "one of the hills" of Moriah strongly suggests that the region of Moriah was not confined to the Temple Mount, but originally encompassed a much larger region. The significance of Jesus crucifixion at this location is not missed by Keil and Delitzsch, who write: "By this event acquires prophetic importance for the Church of the Lord, to which the place of sacrifice points with peculiar clearness, viz., Mount Moriah, upon which under the legal economy all the typical sacrifices were offered to Jehovah; upon which also, in the fulness of time, God the Father gave up His only-begotten Son as an atoning sacrifice for the sins of the whole world, that by this one true sacrifice the shadows of the typical sacrifices might be rendered both real and true. If therefore the appointment of Moriah as the scene of the sacrifice of Isaac, and the offering of a ram in his stead, were primarily only typical in relation to the significance and intent of the Old Testament institution of sacrifice; this type already pointed to the antitype to appear in the future, when the eternal love of the heavenly Father would perform what it had demanded of Abraham; that is to say, when God would not spare His only Son, but give Him up to the real death, which Isaac suffered only in spirit, that we also might die with Christ spiritually, and rise with Him to everlasting life (Rom. 8:32; 6:5, etc.)." (*Pentateuch*, 161–62). For a discussion of the problems associated with identifying Moriah in Genesis 22 with the Moriah of 2 Chr 3:1, see Skinner, *Genesis*, 328–29.

The Ninety-Sixth Thesis

> I will surely bless you and make your descendants as numerous as the stars in the sky and as the sand on the seashore. Your descendants will take possession of the cities of their enemies, and through your offspring all nations on earth will be blessed, because you have obeyed me." (Gen 22:15–18)

How will God bless all people on earth through Abraham? We now have the answer we have been looking for. God is going to reverse the curse and bless all people on earth by sacrificing his only son Jesus, a descendant of Abraham, for the sins of the world. What God only asked Abraham to do with his "only" son is what God always intended to do with his "only" son when he would one day sacrifice Jesus for the sins of the world. It is absolutely no coincidence that the New Testament opens with the words: "This is a book about Jesus Christ the son of David, the *son of Abraham*" (Matt 1:1).[18] The significance of this is not missed by Wright, who writes: "When Matthew announces Jesus as the Messiah, the son of Abraham, then, it means not only that he belongs to that particular people (a real Jew, as we have just seen), but that he belongs to a people whose very reason for existence was to bring blessing to the rest of humanity."[19]

Before concluding this chapter, it is necessary to make one more observation. While the temple of Solomon was a blessing to all people in that it was the place where God and man would be reconciled via the sacrificial system, it left one result of the curse of Genesis unresolved. It did nothing to eliminate the curse of death. Is it merely a coincidence that Jesus offers not only reconciliation with God, but also the promise of eternal life? Only in Jesus is all that was lost in Eden fully restored.

Sometimes when I am by myself, I think about the story of Abraham's sacrifice of Isaac and how it was written so long before Jesus was born and yet bears striking similarities with the story of Christ. Because of the significance of these stories and the remarkable similarities between them, some have suggested that the New Testament writers intentionally shaped the story of Christ to mirror the story of Abraham. However, there are at least three major problems with this suggestion. First, the Old Testament story of Abraham, including both the promises that God made to him and the story of his sacrifice of Isaac, obviously existed long before the time of Jesus and pointed forward to something.[20] The only question is to what? Is an

---

18. Author's translation.
19. Wright, *Knowing Jesus*, 4.
20. The prophecy that concludes that story (Gen 22:14), as well as the promises made

The Story of Abraham

allusion solely to the temple really the best explanation? This interpretation leaves too much unexplained. For example, it does not explain either the peculiar details of the narrative, or why God very specifically asked Abraham to sacrifice his son. The parallels with Christ are much more striking. Second, the New Testament writers do not explain the story of Abraham and Isaac like I do here by drawing parallels between the Old and New Testaments. The most that is said about Abraham and Isaac is recorded in one verse in the book of Hebrews.[21] Thus, the parallels have to be drawn from New Testament books that originally circulated independently, most of which record nothing about Abraham and Isaac. In other words, if the New Testament writers deliberately shaped the story of Jesus to conform to the Old Testament story of Abraham and Isaac, they could have done a much better job! Third, and most telling, many of Jesus' disciples went to their deaths proclaiming that they had seen him alive after his resurrection.[22] For example, Josephus the Jewish historian writes that James the brother of Jesus was stoned to death as a Christian.[23] According to tradition, Peter was crucified upside down and Paul was beheaded. Who would die such painful deaths for something they knew was a lie? It makes absolutely no sense. It all comes down to this: is it more likely that the disciples simply invented these similarities and died for something they knew was a lie, or that those who suggest this are merely grasping for any excuse not to believe that Jesus is the Christ? I will let the reader decide.

---

to Abraham in Gen 12:1–3, reinforce this conclusion.

21. "By faith Abraham, when God tested him, offered Isaac as a sacrifice. He who had received the promise was about to sacrifice his one and only son, even though God had said to him, 'It is through Isaac that your offspring will be reckoned.' Abraham reasoned that that God could raise the dead, and figuratively speaking, he did receive Isaac back from death" (Heb 11:17–19; see also Jas 2:21–23).

22. Because lots of people throughout history have been willing to die for their faith, some have overlooked the significant difference regarding the disciples' willingness to die for their belief in Jesus. J. P. Moreland explains: "The apostles were willing to die for something they had seen with their own eyes and touched with their own hands. They were in a unique position not to just believe Jesus rose from the dead but to know for sure" (Strobel, *Case for Christ*, 247).

23. Josephus, *Antiquities of the Jews*, bk. 20, ch. 9:1.

Conclusion

FIVE HUNDRED YEARS AGO Martin Luther posted his ninety-five grievances to the door of the All Saints Church of Wittenberg and condemned the Catholic Church's sale of indulgences as nothing more than a scheme to raise money for the church. Five hundred years later the church is at it again. This time, however, it is not the Catholic Church that is defrauding the faithful with false promises, but rather evangelical churches. The teaching of indulgences and the teaching of tithing-to-be-blessed are in substance the same and lead to the same result: In both cases, the church walks away with money and the Christian walks away with the equivalent of a promise from a used-car salesman.

This indictment raises four important questions for evangelicals. First, how should evangelical denominations and churches respond to this indictment? Second, how should evangelicals respond to their churches in light of this? Third, how should Christians give if tithing is not incumbent upon the church? Fourth, what is the future of the evangelical movement?

I hope that all evangelical denominations and churches will show some humility and take this criticism both seriously and constructively. Although there are some evangelical churches that do not teach that God blesses the finances of those tithe, many of them do and thus the entire movement must take responsibility. Churches must stop exaggerating the benefits of tithing. There is no promise anywhere in the Bible that God blesses the finances of those who tithe to their local church.

How should evangelicals respond to their churches in light of this indictment? Obviously if churches repent of this teaching, evangelicals should forgive them and move on. Churches are led by people and people make mistakes. It is important to point out that although there are pastors and church leaders who are deliberately taking advantage of others for personal gain, many pastors and church leaders—including the ones

Conclusion

mentioned in chapter 1 of this book—are probably good people who are not intentionally misleading others. They may genuinely believe that God blesses the finances of those who tithe. Their only fault is that they are misinformed. They were born at a time when tithing-to-be-blessed was the tradition and they are merely teaching what they were taught. However, they do not get a free pass for ignorance.[1] There is no evidence that I am aware of that indicates that Luther's antagonist Tetzel was deliberately misleading people either. Tetzel may have genuinely believed in the efficacy of indulgences. Nevertheless, Luther still labeled the sale of indulgences as nothing more than a scheme to fill the coffers of the church.[2] It makes no difference to God whether someone is taking advantage of others wittingly or unwittingly. People are being taken advantage of in God's name and God cannot be happy about this. Churches should not be raising money with the sales techniques of the business world. Churches must be held to a higher standard if for no other reason than that they represent the one with the highest of standards.

If tithing is not incumbent upon the church, how then should Christians give? The obvious answer is that they should give according to the principles laid out in the New Testament. There are three of them. First, Christians should give expecting to get nothing in return. This is what Jesus taught in Luke 6:35, when he said: "But love your enemies, do good to them, and lend to them *without expecting to get anything back*." Ironically this is the exact opposite of the teaching of evangelical churches which encourage Christians to give to get more! If Jesus taught us to give to our enemies without expecting anything in return, then surely this should be our attitude when giving to God.

Second, Christians should give in secret. Jesus said:

> Be careful not to do your "acts of righteousness" before men, to be seen by them. If you do, you will have no reward from your Father in heaven. So when you give to the needy, do not announce it with trumpets, as the hypocrites do in the synagogues and on the streets, to be honored by men. I tell you the truth, they have

---

1. Leaders have a responsibility to make sure they know what they are talking about. The fact that this has gone on for so long tells me that many do not examine their own teachings in the light of scripture. The fact that some may genuinely believe that God blesses the finances of those who tithe means nothing to me because, as we learned in chapter 4, people can talk themselves into anything they want to believe, especially if they benefit from it in some way.

2. Kittelson, *Luther the Reformer*, 124.

received their reward in full. But when you give to the needy, do not let your left hand know what your right hand is doing, so that your giving may be in secret. Then your Father, who sees what is done in secret, will reward you. (Matt 6:1–4)

Why did Jesus insist that his followers give in secret? Because he knew all the problems that would result from people not giving secretly. He knew that some people would give not because they care, but only because they want it to appear that they care. As history has advanced, other problems with public giving have come to light. Some pastors and church leaders use their knowledge of who gives what for personal gain. Others show favoritism to those who give the most. Others use tithing as a measure of spiritual growth. Ironically, all these problems could be avoided if people followed Jesus' command to give in secret.

Lastly, Christians should give cheerfully in accordance with what they can afford. Paul says that Christians should be cheerful givers (2 Cor 9:7). Notice that Paul did not say that Christians should be cheerful tithers. How can anyone give cheerfully when there is already an expectation that they should give a certain percentage?

Christians who give in accordance with these principles must be aware that they are going to face a lot of resistance from church leaders who naturally want to know who gives what to the church and even encourage that with their system of offering envelopes. Of course, church leaders will insist that these envelopes are used for tax purposes. While that may be true, they are also used as a convenient way to record who gives what to the church. I would encourage those Christians who want to give in complete secrecy to avoid using these envelopes, give up the tax deduction, and give only in cash. There are two advantages to this. First, it is the only way to give in absolute secrecy; it is the only way to ensure that no one knows who gives what to the church. Second, it allows every individual the freedom to give cheerfully an amount he or she can afford.

If we sincerely believe in God and truly care about others, then evangelical churches are going to have to make some changes. Far too many churches have become businesses first and churches second. Like politicians who are naturally inclined toward self-preservation, too many pastors and church leaders seem more concerned with their professional survival than with the gospel. There are a lot of problems in the world and so many of them go back to one thing, money! Paul said that it is the love of money that is the root of all evil (1 Tim 6:10). What was Luther's problem with indulgences?

Conclusion

It was a scheme to raise money for the church. What is the problem with the teaching of tithing-to-be-blessed? It is a scheme to raise money for the church. If we are ever going to truly reform churches, we must find ways to diminish the influence of money.[3] The future of the evangelical movement, in my view, rests not on the shoulders of those who want a good job in a nice building with a good salary, but on volunteers who will preach the gospel the way Paul did, freely and because they care. This means that, at least in some instances, there is going to have to be a transition away from full-time ministers who earn a salary to bi-vocational or even volunteer pastors who are willing to preach the gospel anywhere, including in home churches.[4] Too much money is going to fund buildings and not enough is going to make an impact upon the world. In his *Sermon on Indulgence and Grace*, Luther reminds us that it is much better to help those in need than to give to a building.[5] Does this mean that churches should be torn down, or that no pastor should ever be paid? Of course not. However, it would be better to tear all of them down and not pay another salary than to manipulate people into giving money on the basis of false promises. I would much rather have a home church that is built upon a foundation of truth, than a megachurch that is built upon a foundation of lies.

The popularity of tithing-to-be-blessed among evangelical ministers is no doubt to some degree due to the fact that many churches are struggling financially. Many pastors genuinely fear that their churches would not survive if they stopped teaching their congregations to tithe. It is important to reiterate that tithing is not the problem. The teaching of tithing-to-be-blessed *is* the problem. Churches are still free to ask Christians to tithe, but they must do so without making misleading promises. I think the best

---

3. Bright writes: "A church which has no rebuke for society, which demands lavish support before righteous behavior, is no true church but a sham of a church" (*Kingdom of God*, 62).

4. Paul makes it clear that the church is not a building or a group of buildings but the body of all believers in Jesus Christ throughout all ages (1 Cor 12:12–31; Eph 4:1–16). This means that church can be held anywhere two or more people gather together in God's name, including in houses. If the early church met in houses, why is it difficult for modern Christians to do this? I think that this would be particularly ideal for small churches that no longer receive adequate funding. There would certainly be some advantages to this. The most obvious one is financial. Meeting in homes would eliminate virtually all overhead. Christians could then use their resources to help those in need, rather than simply paying bills. Another advantage of home church is that the smaller setting would force people to build relationships. Is that not what life is all about?

5. Pettegree, *Brand Luther*, 80.

The Ninety-Sixth Thesis

approach is for church leaders to be honest with their congregations and to remind them that churches need money to survive. I sense that some church leaders fear that if they did this, they would receive less money. Ironically, it is often those who are supposed to have the most faith that sometimes have the least faith! While they might receive less from a few, it is also very possible that they might receive more from many. By removing the compulsion to tithe, those who give little to nothing now might actually want to give more. I'm reminded of the words of Paul: "The letter kills, but the Spirit gives life" (2 Cor 3:6).

I hope that this indictment does not overshadow the positive message of this book, which is that there is a God whose role in the world can be discerned by those who diligently seek him. The Bible encourages us to seek God. This implies that there must be clues somewhere. The second half of this book is about finding those clues. Ironically, the more I lost faith in the church, the more I found faith in Christ. The reason for this is that I began finding answers to some of the most perplexing questions about God.

One of the reasons people do not believe in God has to do with the disconnect between the Bible and reality. Miracles do not seem to be happening at all, let alone with the same degree of frequency and intensity as in New Testament times. However, we learned in chapter 2 that there is a reason for this and that reason is found in the close relationship between Jesus' miracles and his announcement of the arrival of the kingdom of God. When Jesus was here two thousand years ago, he performed miracles to validate his claim that God's kingdom had arrived on earth. How would people know that the kingdom of God had arrived? Because of the miracles that Jesus performed. The miracles were signs of the dawning of a new age; signs that God's kingdom had broken into the world and that the world was now a different place. However, we should not expect these miracles today because Jesus and his kingdom are no longer here, they are yet to come (Matt 6:10). Once Jesus died on the cross and returned to the father, it could no longer be said that the kingdom of God had arrived, but that the kingdom of God will arrive. The miracles that Jesus and his disciples performed were merely a foretaste of the goodness to come when Jesus returns at the end of the age.

Although Jesus performed miracles to validate his claim that God's kingdom had arrived on earth, for some reason he went out of his way to prevent the vast majority of people from discovering that he was a miracle worker. The reason for this, according to chapter 3, is that he did not want

Conclusion

those outside of his inner circle of disciples to know that he was the long-anticipated Jewish Messiah. This explains why he spoke plainly to the disciples, but in strange parables to everyone else. The reason for this is very insightful. Jesus came to earth with a very specific plan and that plan was to die on the cross for the sins of the world. Had too many witnessed his miracles, they would have discovered his identity and never have allowed the miracle-working Messiah to accomplish his mission.

This insight that Jesus had a plan and that everything he did was subordinate to this plan is one of the most important insights of this book because it holds the clue to answering some of the most elusive questions about God. Why does God not reveal himself in an undeniable way? Why does God not immediately eliminate all evil? Why does God not get more involved in the world's affairs? Because doing these things would interfere with his plan which requires that he keep his existence a secret. Just as Jesus was limited by his plan, God is limited by his plan. It is his plan, not his power, that prevents him from doing all the good that we would otherwise expect him to do.

In chapter 4, we learned that God reveals himself as a God who defies human wisdom. Sometimes God defies human wisdom by doing things in unexpected ways, such as when he gave Abraham and Sarah a child in their old age. Other times, God defies human wisdom by accomplishing his will through weak and ineffectual individuals. Either way, the point is the same: Nothing is impossible for God! Thus, we must not only approach God with a certain amount of humility because we are dealing with a being who is completely different from us, but we must also be extremely cautious about drawing conclusions about what is or is not possible on the basis of our limited experience. Humans in their arrogance are being baited into a trap and it is the God who defies human wisdom who has set the bait.

Finally, this book closed with the story of Abraham which not only sets the stage for what the Bible is all about, but also offers one of the most compelling reasons to believe that the Bible is indeed the word of God and that Jesus is the Christ. Here in the Old Testament, hundreds of years before Jesus was a born, is a story remarkably similar to the New Testament story, a story about another Father who would one day offer his "only" son for the sins of the world.

This book leaves the reader with a very important question. Is everything that we see really the result of one big accident, as we have been indirectly taught, or is it the result of an elaborate plan weaved in the mind of

The Ninety-Sixth Thesis

a God whose ways we simply do not understand? To at least some of those who argue the former the answer is so obvious that they can only ridicule those who believe in God and dismiss them as adults who still believe in fairy tales. After all, miracles do not seem to be happening today. The fraud and deceit of modern-day faith healers only reinforces this conclusion. Second, God's existence is not so obvious that it cannot be denied. Third, there is evil in the world and little to no evidence of any divine intervention to stop it. What this book has argued, however, is not that these observations are incorrect, but that our assumptions about God are incorrect.[6] People assume that if God exists, he would want his existence to be obvious. People assume that if God exists, he would immediately eliminate every trace of evil. People assume that if God exists, he would end inequality and poverty and stop hurricanes. The problem is that all of these things just might be part of the divine plan, a plan spun in the mind of a God who put us on earth not simply to be happy and to live it up, but for something much deeper and far more significant.

The British philosopher and atheist Bertrand Russell was once asked the question what he would say to God if, after death, he discovered that God exists. Russell replied: "Not enough evidence, God, not enough evidence!"[7] Behind Russell's response lies one of these incorrect assumptions. He assumes that God would want his existence to be more obvious than it is. However, God's existence is not obvious, but now we know why. It was not supposed to be! That was never part of the divine plan.

---

6. This argument opens up an entirely new range of possibilities for our thinking about God. The simple thoughts about God, such as there is evil in the world therefore God must not exist, are going to have to be jettisoned in favor of thoughts that are based upon much deeper thinking. If a God such as the one who reveals himself in the Bible exists, then anything is possible, including that he is making sport of us, especially those of us who deny his existence. Something must explain all of this. The idea that all of this just happened by chance—the reproductive organs, the eyes, taste buds, etc.—is simply hard to believe. It makes no difference to me if someone believes in evolution. What is absurd is the idea that all of this just happened by chance! The book of Proverbs says: "There is a way that seems right to a man, but in the end it leads to death" (Prov 14:12). If our assumptions about God are incorrect then we are going to have to start giving consideration to ideas about God that at one time would have been considered unthinkable, including the possibility that the world was setup to have problems. If there were just one person on earth, there would be few problems because all the resources would belong to that one person. But when you put seven billion people on one planet with limited resources, it seems that the world was deliberately setup to have problems. As chapter 3 argued, problems just might be part of the divine plan!

7. Salmon, "Religion and Science," 176.

Conclusion

I want to conclude this book with an honest and authentic discussion about God that answers three questions. What is the gospel of Jesus Christ? What expectations should Christians have for God in the present life? And finally, what is God's plan for us and why are we here?

The biggest problem with the evangelical teaching of tithing-to-be-blessed is not simply that Christians are being taken advantage of, but that they are being misled with respect to what the Christian life is about. The word gospel derives from a Greek word that means "good news." What is the good news of the gospel of Jesus Christ? Popular Christian books promote a gospel of health, wealth, and happiness. Wilkinson's *The Prayer of Jabez* and the many books by Joel Osteen are examples of this.[8] The popularity of these books and others like them is that they tell people what they want to hear. However, that is precisely what makes their teachings unlikely to be true. If we are really interested in the truth, it is not likely to be found in what we want to hear, but in what we do not want to hear. Before explaining what the good news of the gospel of Jesus Christ is, it may be helpful to explain what it is not.

The gospel of Jesus Christ has nothing to do with health. If God allowed John the Baptist to be beheaded (Matt 14:1–12), Stephen to be stoned to death (Acts 7:54–60), and his own son to be crucified at Calvary, does it really make sense that the gospel of Jesus Christ is a gospel that promises health? If God allowed such horrible things to happen to his most faithful and loyal servants in the Bible, why should modern, typically Western, Christians think that the gospel of Jesus Christ is a gospel of health?

The gospel of Jesus Christ has nothing to do with wealth. Once again, the lives of the men and women we read about in the Bible are instructive. With few exceptions, most of the people we read about in the Bible were extremely poor. John the Baptist lived in the desert and ate locusts and wild honey (Matt 3:4). The old woman whom Jesus praised for giving her only two coins to the temple treasury was extremely poor (Mark 12:41–44). The Apostle Paul was also poor (2 Cor 6:10). Again, we must ask, if God did not make his most loyal servants in the Bible wealthy, why should modern Christians believe that God wants them to be wealthy?

The gospel of Jesus Christ has nothing to do with happiness. We live in a postmodern world that teaches that the only truth is what makes us

---

8. Wilkinson's *Prayer of Jabez* teaches that God wants Christians to pray selfishly and to pray for God's blessing for themselves first (Wilkinson, *Prayer of Jabez*, 18–19).

The Ninety-Sixth Thesis

happy. "Happiness is the Truth," according to one popular song.[9] Many in the church seem to believe this too. But this belief does not conform with what we read in the Bible either. For example, the children of Israel were slaves in Egypt for four hundred years. For four hundred years the Hebrews were born into slavery and died in slavery. No amount of prayer could have changed their situation because this was part of God's plan.[10] If God's objective was to make the Hebrew slaves happy, he failed miserably. But it is not just the Hebrew slaves who had difficult lives, but virtually every one of the men and women we read about in the Bible. Jeremiah's life as a prophet was so bad that he cursed the day he was born! His words are recorded in Jer 20:14–18:

> Cursed be the day I was born! May the day my mother bore me not be blessed! Cursed be the man who brought my father the news, who made him very glad, saying, "A child is born to you—a son!" May that man be like the towns the LORD overthrew without pity. May he hear wailing in the morning, a battle cry at noon. For he did not kill me in the womb, with my mother as my grave, her womb enlarged forever. Why did I ever come out of the womb to see trouble and sorrow and to end my days in shame?

Does this sound like a man who is happy? I have often wondered how Jeremiah or John the Baptist, who was imprisoned waiting for the executioner, would respond to Osteen who paraphrases God when he writes: "You need to get ready. I have explosive blessings coming your way. Where you are is not permanent. I will take you higher. I will increase you beyond your normal income. I will bless you beyond your salary. I will suddenly change things for the better in your life."[11] But things do not always get better, as the story of John the Baptist's beheading illustrates. There are true and false prophets today, just as there were in biblical times. The problem

---

9. Pharrell Williams, "Happy," track 5 on *Girl* (Columbia Records, 2014). See also Sheryl Crow, "If It Makes You Happy," track 5 on *Sheryl Crow* (A&M Records, 1996). The arts in general and songs in particular are windows into culture that tell us what people are thinking at the time. These songs and others like them show the influence of postmodernism.

10. Years earlier God had told Abram that his descendants would be slaves in Egypt for a period of four hundred years (Gen 15:13). The Hebrews were a mere seventy people at the time Jacob and his family migrated to Egypt (Exod 1:1–5). God's plan required that he keep them within the confines of Egypt until they grew into a mighty nation large enough to take on the inhabitants of Canaan.

11. Osteen, *Breakout!*, 39.

Conclusion

has always been how to distinguish between them. Fortunately, there is a way to distinguish between them. False prophets tell people what they want to hear, while true prophets tell people what they do not want to hear.

John the Baptist and Jeremiah were also not alone in their suffering. The book of Hebrews records some of the sufferings experienced by some of God's other faithful servants:

> Some faced jeers and flogging, while still others were chained and put in prison. They were stoned; they were sawed in two; they were put to death by the sword. They went about in sheepskins and goatskins, destitute, persecuted and mistreated—the world was not worthy of them. They wandered in deserts and mountains, and in caves and holes in the ground. These were all commended for their faith, yet none of them received what had been promised. God had planned something better for us so that only together with us would they be made perfect. (Heb 11:36-40)

It is impossible to read the entire Bible and conclude that the gospel of Jesus Christ is about happiness. Only a superficial reading of it could lead to such a conclusion. But this raises an important question. If the gospel of Jesus Christ is not about health, wealth, and happiness, what is it about? A clue is in v. 39 of the scripture cited above: "none of them received what had been promised." What is that they were promised? Before answering this question, it is imperative that we briefly discuss one of the most ignored topics of the New Testament.

The New Testament says a lot about a topic that few of us want to talk about—namely, suffering. For obvious reasons, this topic is conveniently left out of church sermons. After all, who wants to hear about suffering? However, it is impossible to understand the good news of the gospel of Jesus Christ without understanding this important topic.

When God told Ananias to go and lay hands upon Paul, Ananias was naturally reluctant to go because he had heard many bad reports about Paul (Acts 9:13-14). God then responded to Ananias with these strange words that are completely at odds with human wisdom: "Go! This man is my chosen instrument to carry my name before the Gentiles and their kings and before the people of Israel. *I will show him how much he must suffer for my name*" (Acts 9:15-16). What did God mean by this? Did God want Paul to suffer? This does not sound anything like the popular version of the gospel that is proclaimed in many evangelical churches. In 2 Corinthians Paul recorded some of the sufferings he experienced as an ambassador of Christ:

The Ninety-Sixth Thesis

Are they servants of Christ? (I am out of my mind to talk like this) I am more. I have worked much harder, been in prison more frequently, been flogged more severely, and been exposed to death again and again. Five times I received from the Jews the forty lashes minus one. Three times I was beaten with rods, once I was stoned, three times I was shipwrecked, I spent a night and a day in the open sea, I have been constantly on the move. I have been in danger from rivers, in danger from bandits, in danger from my own countrymen, in danger from Gentiles; in danger in the city, in danger in the country, in danger at sea; and in danger from false brothers. I have labored and toiled and have often gone without sleep; I have known hunger and thirst and have often gone without food; I have been cold and naked. (2 Cor 11:23–27)

But what is really remarkable about Paul is not only that he was willing to suffer so much for Christ, but that he rejoiced in those sufferings (Rom 5:3 and Col 1:24). He wrote to the Philippian church: "I want to know Christ and the power of his resurrection *and the fellowship of sharing in his sufferings*" (Phil 3:10). Paul also taught that it was the duty of every Christian to share in the sufferings of Christ. "For it has been granted to you on behalf of Christ not only to believe on him, but also to suffer for him" (Phil 1:29). On one occasion Paul was stoned and left for dead. The next day he got up and said the following words which completely defy human wisdom: "With such sufferings it is necessary to enter the kingdom of God" (Acts 14:22). I cannot help but think that we can learn a lot from this man.

The observation that the gospel of Jesus Christ is a gospel for those who suffer does not necessarily mean that God wants people to suffer, only that a certain amount of suffering is inevitable in this life. There is no such thing as a perfect life. Even if you could conceptualize the perfect life, it would still not be perfect because it has to end. Life is not easy, but now we know why. It was not intended to be. Jesus admitted this when he said: "In this world you will have trouble" (John 16:33).

The observation that the gospel of Jesus Christ is a gospel for the suffering helps us to understand why many evangelical churches have transformed the gospel of Jesus Christ into something else. It is becoming increasingly clear that over the last seventy years, the gospel of Jesus Christ has been confused and conflated with the American dream. The reason for this is obvious. The gospel of the American dream is the kind of gospel that people naturally want to hear. It gets people into churches and, most importantly, gets people to give money. It is much easier to sell a gospel of

Conclusion

health, wealth, and happiness than a gospel that offers very little in the present life. The truth is that God promises no one a good life here on earth, let alone health, wealth, and happiness. The good news of the gospel of Jesus Christ is in one promise, a better life is coming!

A while back, I read a comment to an article on tithing by a man who claimed to have tithed faithfully his entire adult life. This same man also claimed to have always helped those in financial need. He then went on to express his frustration with tithing because he himself was now in financial need and there were no unexpected checks arriving in his mailbox. He concluded that he no longer trusts God for anything other than the promise of eternal life. He suddenly knew what every Christian should have known all along and that is that the only promise that the gospel of Jesus Christ promises anyone is the promise of eternal life.[12] However, there is at least one advantage to this.

We live in a pluralistic society where there are many religions and it is often very difficult to distinguish between their vastly different truth claims. This is especially challenging in light of the observation that there is a lot of good in most religions and that at least some of their teachings overlap.[13] However, there is at least one way to distinguish between the competing truths claims of the various religions. If a religious teaching appeals to my human desires, I know it is not likely to be true. Why? Because if it appeals to my human desires, the more likely it was made up. Humans often take advantage of others by telling them what they want to hear. The church's teaching of tithing-to-be-blessed is a perfect example of this. After all, who does not want to hear that God wants them to be wealthy? If, on the other hand, a religious teaching does not appeal to my human desires, I know that it is much more likely to be true. Paul's teaching that suffering is a necessary component of the Christian life does not appeal to me at all, but

---

12. A caveat is necessary here. I am not saying that God does not bless us in the present life. He certainly does. The Bible considers the sun and rain blessings (Matt 5:45). However, many of the blessings experienced in this life are somewhat random and certainly not experienced equally by everyone. Just being born at a particular place and at a particular time in history can be either a blessing or a curse. Imagine being born a Jew in Poland in the 1920s! The only blessing that we are all promised equally is the promise of eternal life.

13. C.S. Lewis has an interesting perspective on religions. He writes: "Being a Christian does mean thinking that where Christianity differs from other religions, Christianity is right and they are wrong. As in arithmetic—there is only one right answer to a sum, and all other answers are wrong: but some of the wrong answers are much nearer being right than others" (*Mere Christianity*, 43).

that is precisely what makes the Christian message believable. The gospel of Jesus Christ is a gospel that is not likely to have been made up because it is a gospel that does not appeal to our earthly desires.

There may be some who are disappointed with the conclusion that the gospel of Jesus Christ promises nothing other than eternal life through Jesus Christ. Some might even ask why they should serve a God who does not promise health, wealth, and happiness. But it is this question that reveals the problem with humanity. This is a very selfish question; we humans are very selfish. If we stop and think about it, practically every bad behavior derives from selfishness. It is obvious that murder, rape, adultery, and theft all derive from selfishness, but so do many of the lesser sins like envy, jealousy, greed, and hatred.

One of the things I appreciate about the Bible is its honesty. The New Testament freely admits that Jesus' disciples struggled with selfishness, just like we do. On one occasion, two of them came to Jesus privately and asked him for positions of power when he returns with his kingdom (Mark 10:35–37). Naturally, when the other disciples found out about this, they were indignant. Jesus then used this as an opportunity to teach them a valuable lesson. He said: "You know that the rulers of the Gentiles lord it over them, and their high officials exercise authority over them. Not so with you. Instead, whoever wants to become great among you must be your servant, and whoever wants to be first must be your slave—just as the Son of Man did not come to be served, but to serve, and to give his life as a ransom for many" (Matt 20:25–28). I get the impression that what would have really pleased Jesus is if these same two disciples would have come to him seeking those positions of power for someone other than themselves.

The observation that we humans are selfish perhaps holds the clue to understanding why we are here. The Bible says that God created man for his pleasure (Rev 4:11). But what pleasure could God possibly find in us? The answer must be that God, like most parents, gets pleasure watching his children transform from the selfish people that they were born into the unselfish people that he wants them to become.

In an earlier chapter, we learned that there are a lot of lessons in life for those who are paying attention. I suggested that the reason God does not eliminate evil is because we learn from it. It teaches us something about the human condition, namely that the Bible's assessment of the human heart is exactly right (Jer 17:9). God wants us to see what humans are capable of. But these life lessons are not limited to evil. They are everywhere and

Conclusion

touch on a variety of topics. Whether I am reading history or the news or simply observing human behavior, I am learning something about humanity. Every day I make observations that teach me valuable life lessons that reinforce the conclusion that someone is trying to teach me something. Again, who could that be but God? A few examples will suffice.

People are constantly trying to promote the idea that money and power are what matters in life. However, there are so many life lessons that contradict this. How many powerful people—political figures, entertainers, and athletes—have come and gone in our brief lifetimes? I can think of many whose careers started long after I was born and not only are their careers long over, but they are already gone. God expects us to make these observations and learn from them. What could be the lesson here but that it does not matter who we are or what we have, we will not be here very long. It was observations like these that made me carefully consider the truth claims of the Bible.

Although we are all human and we all desire money, most of us betray an awareness that there are things in life far more important than money. One of these is relationships. Anytime people discuss what is really important to them, relationships are always at the top of the list. How many times have we seen a long-running television series come to an end, only to see the actors and actresses express deep sadness? It is not the work that they are going to miss, as much as the people with whom they worked. Someone once said, and I think correctly, if there is a clue to the meaning of life, it is in relationships.[14]

A few years ago, I had a minor plumbing problem in my house. My father was a plumber so I naturally called him for advice. A week or so later I called him back to tell him that I fixed the problem. On the phone that day, he thanked me for sending him some money that I had sent him to buy groceries. He had been sick and unable to work. He then informed me that he had no intentions of spending that money. I told him that I wanted him to spend it and reminded him of all the times that he helped me. He suddenly became very authentic with me and told me something that I would never have known. He said, "To be honest, Brian, when I received the money and the nice letter that you wrote with it, I actually broke down and cried." I never heard my father be so authentic. I told him that I loved him and hung up the phone. Little did I know that would be the last conversation that I would ever have with my father. A few days later, my wife

---

14. Ravi Zacharias is to be credited with this thought. The exact source is unknown.

called me at work. She was crying and told me that my father had passed away. It was not long before I thought back to our last conversation and recalled those final words with my father. I could not help but think that last conversation was a blessing from God and another reminder of what is really important in life.

When I was in graduate school, a friend and I were discussing how fortunate we were to have received full academic scholarships to pursue PhDs. Other students were even more fortunate and received stipends to help them with their living expenses. I lived off campus and had a good job so I did not need this extra money, but my friend did. He and his family really could have benefited from it. But he said something to me that day that I have never forgotten. In a very sincere manner, he simply said: "God did not have that for me." He was not angry or upset. He was not jealous that others got something that he did not. He was simply thankful for what God had given him. But I learned something from him that day. Here was an unselfish human. I cannot help but think that God must want all of our attitudes to be like his. Although we are all different and we all experience the world differently, I would imagine that we all have stories like these. Someone is trying to teach us to become better people and to value the things that are really important in life and that someone is a lot like the God of the Bible. But these life lessons must not be viewed as an end, but as a means to an end. What could be the purpose of these life lessons but that we change?

One of the observations I have made is that we all have regrets in life. What must not be overlooked is what these regrets teach us. What do regrets teach us but that we have changed? I have often wondered if God is not going to use these regrets as a measure of just how much we have changed. Regrets are evidence of the amazing transformation that takes place over our lifetimes. We should not be the same people at the end of our lives as we were at the beginning. God expects us to change and to transform. Just as parents expect their kids to change over time, God expects us to change and to transform over the course of our lives. But what does God want us to transform into? We have already made the observation that we humans are very selfish. I must confess that I never would have noticed this in others if I had not noticed it in myself first. Some might argue that they are not selfish or that they know someone who is not selfish. However, it is not so much the selfish acts that we have done that are the problem, but the selfish acts that we are all capable of that are the problem. Under the right

Conclusion

circumstances, we are all capable of the most egregious forms of selfishness. However, because God is different from us, I would expect him to be unselfish. It is no coincidence that Jesus Christ is the paragon of unselfishness. It was Jesus, the king of all the universe, who said that he did not come to be served, but to serve and to give his life as a ransom for many (Matt 20:28; Mark 10:45). God created us not simply to become unselfish, but to believe in and ultimately become more like his son. But such a radical transformation is not easy. I am reminded of a quote from Tolstoy: "Everyone thinks of changing the world, but no one thinks of changing himself."[15]

The older I become the less impressed I am with the things that impressed me in my youth. I am no longer impressed with sports because I realize that so much of it is based on luck. What really impresses me is when I see humans do things that go against the natural human inclination for self-preservation. The names of William Tyndale, Corrie ten Boom and Oskar Schindler immediately come to mind. Tyndale was strangled and then burned at the stake for translating the Bible into English.[16] His last words were not an appeal for himself, but an appeal to God to open the king of England's eyes to permit the Bible to be written in English.[17] A short time later, God answered Tyndale's prayer and the king permitted the Bible to be translated into English.[18] Ten Boom and Schindler risked their lives to hide Jews, a people the Nazis considered to be subhuman. I cannot help but think that we can learn a lot from such people. They were a lot more like Christ than most of us who profess his name, whether they knew it or not.

---

15. Quoted in Bryan et al., *Artist's Way at Work*, 160.
16. Lane, "William Tyndale," 204.
17. Lane, "William Tyndale," 204.
18. Lane, "William Tyndale," 205.

Bibliography

Albright, W. F. *Archaeology and the Religion of Ancient Israel*. Louisville: Westminster John Knox, 2006.
Alcorn, Randy. *The Treasure Principle*. Sisters, OR: Multnomah, 2001.
Alexander, T. D. *From Paradise to the Promised Land: An Introduction to the Pentateuch*. Grand Rapids: Paternoster, 2002.
Alter, Robert. *The Art of Biblical Narrative*. New York: Basic, 1981.
Anderson, Bernhard W. *Understanding the Old Testament*. Englewood Cliffs, NJ: Prentice-Hall, 1986.
Bakker, Jim. *I Was Wrong: The Untold Story of the Shocking Journey from PTL Power to Prison and Beyond*. Nashville: Nelson, 1996.
Barthes, Roland. "The Death of the Author." In *The Rustle of Language*, translated by Richard Howard, 49–55. New York: Hill and Wang, 1986.
Beitzel, Barry J. *The Moody Atlas of Bible Lands*. Chicago: Moody, 1985.
Bowler, Kate. *Blessed: A History of the American Prosperity Gospel*. Oxford: Oxford University Press, 2013.
Bright, John. *A History of Israel*. Louisville: Westminster John Knox, 2000.
———. *The Kingdom of God*. Nashville: Abingdon, 1981.
Bryan, Mark A., et al. *The Artist's Way at Work: Riding the Dragon*. New York: Morrow, 1998.
Bultmann, Rudolf. "New Testament and Mythology." In *Kerygma and Myth: A Theological Debate*, edited by H. W. Bartsch, translated by R. H. Fuller, 1–44. New York: Harper & Row, 1961.
Carroll, James. *Christ Actually: Reimagining Faith in the Modern Age*. New York: Penguin, 2014.
Cassuto, Umberto. *The Documentary Hypothesis and the Composition of the Pentateuch*. Jerusalem: Magnes, 1961.
Collins, Kenneth J. *The Evangelical Movement: The Promise of an American Religion*. Grand Rapids: Baker Academic, 2005.
Cranfield, C. E. B. *The Gospel according to St Mark*. Cambridge: Cambridge University Press, 1959.
Cross, Frank Moore, Jr. *The Ancient Library of Qumran & Modern Biblical Studies*. Grand Rapids: Baker, 1980.
Dana, H. E., and Julius R. Mantey. *A Manual Grammar of the New Testament*. Upper Saddle River, NJ: Prentice Hall, 1955.
Hamilton, Victor P. *The Book of Genesis*. Grand Rapids: Eerdmans, 1995.

Bibliography

Harrell, David Edwin, Jr. *All Things Are Possible: The Healing & Charismatic Revivals in Modern America*. Bloomington: Indiana University Press, 1975.

———. *Oral Roberts: An American Life*. Bloomington: Indiana University Press, 1985.

Hoffmeier, James K. *Ancient Israel in Sinai: The Evidence for the Authenticity of the Wilderness Tradition*. New York: Oxford University Press, 2005.

———. *Israel in Egypt: The Evidence for the Authenticity of the Exodus Tradition*. New York: Oxford University Press, 1996.

———. "'These Things Happened': Why a Historical Exodus Is Essential for Theology." In *Do Historical Matters Matter to Faith?*, edited by James K. Hoffmeier and Dennis R. Magary, 99–134. Wheaton, IL: Crossway, 2012.

Hood, Kregg. *Take God at His Word: Experience the Power of Giving*. Canada, 2009.

Hudnut-Beumler, James. *In Pursuit of the Almighty's Dollar: A History of Money and American Protestantism*. Chapel Hill: University of North Carolina Press, 2007.

———. *Looking for God in the Suburbs: The Religion of the American Dream and Its Critics, 1945–1965*. New Jersey: Rutgers University Press, 1994.

Iacocca, Lee. *Where Have All the Leaders Gone?* New York: Scribner, 2007.

Janis, Irving. *Groupthink: Psychological Studies of Policy Decisions and Fiascoes*. Boston: Houghton Mifflin, 1982.

Jones, David W., and Russell S. Woodbridge. *Health, Wealth & Happiness*. Grand Rapids: Kregel, 2011.

Kaiser, Walter C., Jr. *The Messiah in the Old Testament*. Grand Rapids: Zondervan, 1995.

Keil, C. F., and F. Delitzsch. *1 & 2 Kings, 1 & 2 Chronicles*. Translated by James Martin. Peabody: Hendrickson, 2011.

———. *Pentateuch*. Translated by James Martin. Peabody: Hendrickson, 2011.

Kelly, Russell Earl. *Should the Church Teach Tithing? A Theologian's Conclusions about a Taboo Doctrine*. New York: Writer's Club, 2007.

Kitchen, K. A. *On the Reliability of the Old Testament*. Grand Rapids: Eerdmans, 2003.

Kittelson, James M. *Luther the Reformer: The Story of the Man and His Career*. Minneapolis: Fortress, 2003.

Lane, A. N. S. "William Tyndale." In *Great Leaders of the Christian Church*, edited by John D. Woodbridge, 202–5. Chicago: Moody, 1988.

Lehmann, Chris. *The Money Cult: Capitalism, Christianity, and the Unmaking of the American Dream*. Brooklyn, NY: Melville House, 2016.

Lewis, C. S. *Mere Christianity*. New York: Macmillan, 1952.

Long, V. Phillips. "The Art of Biblical History." In *Foundations of Contemporary Interpretation*, edited by Moises Silva, 287–429. Grand Rapids: Zondervan, 1996.

Ludwig, Theodore M. *The Sacred Paths of the West*. 3rd ed. Upper Saddle River, NJ: Pearson Prentice Hall, 2006.

McKenzie, Steven L., and Stephen R. Haynes, eds. *To Each Its Own Meaning*. Louisville: Westminster John Knox, 1999.

Melchert, Norman. *The Great Conversation: A Historical Introduction to Philosophy*. 4th ed. Oxford: Oxford University Press, 2002.

Miller, Donald E., and Tetsunao Yamamori, *Global Pentecostalism: The New Face of Christian Social Engagement*. Berkeley: University of California Press, 2007.

Miller, J. Maxwell. "Reading the Bible Historically: The Historian's Approach." In *To Each Its Own Meaning*, edited by Steven L. McKenzie and Stephen R. Haynes, 17–34. Louisville: Westminster John Knox Press, 1999.

Bibliography

Miller, Timothy. *The Hippies and American Values.* Knoxville: University of Tennessee Press, 1991.

Nolen, William A. *Healing: A Doctor in Search of a Miracle.* New York: Random House, 1974.

Osteen, Joel. *Breakout! 5 Keys to Go beyond Your Barriers and Live an Extraordinary Life.* New York: FaithWords, 2013.

———. *The Power of I Am: Two Words That Will Change Your Life Today.* New York: FaithWords, 2015.

Pettegree, Andrew. *Brand Luther.* New York: Penguin, 2015.

Powers, Kirsten. *The Silencing: How the Left Is Killing Free Speech.* Washington, DC: Regnery, 2015.

Rainer, Art. *The Money Challenge: 30 Days of Discovering God's Design for You and Your Money.* Nashville: B & H, 2017.

Ramsey, Dave. *Dave Ramsey's Complete Guide to Money.* Brentwood, TN: Lampo, 2011.

Randi, James. *The Faith Healers.* New York: Prometheus, 1989.

Reich, Charles A. *The Greening of America.* New York: Random House, 1970.

Salmon, Wesley C. "Religion and Science: A New Look at Hume's Dialogues." *Philosophical Studies* 33 (1978) 143–76.

Segal, M. H. *The Pentateuch: Its Composition and Its Authorship and Other Biblical Studies.* Jerusalem: Magnes, 1967.

Skinner, John. *A Critical and Exegetical Commentary on Genesis.* Edinburgh: T. & T. Clark, 1910.

Smietana, Bob. "Prosperity Gospel Taught to 4 in 10 Evangelical Churchgoers." *Christianity Today*, July 31, 2018. https://www.christianitytoday.com/news/2018/july/prosperity-gospel-survey-churchgoers-prosper-tithe-blessing.html.

Storr, Vernon F. *From Abraham to Christ: Studies in the Development of the Theism of the Old Testament.* Warburton Lectures 1923–1927. Garden City: Doubleday, 1928.

Strobel, Lee. *The Case for Christ: A Journalist's Personal Investigation of the Evidence for Jesus.* Grand Rapids: Zondervan, 1998.

Tozer, A. W. *The Pursuit of God.* Camphill, PA: Christian Publications, 1993.

Vanhoozer, Kevin J. *Is There a Meaning in This Text: The Bible, the Reader, and the Morality of Literary Knowledge.* Grand Rapids: Zondervan, 1998.

Vos, Howard F. *Exploring Church History.* Nashville: Nelson, 1994.

Wells, H. G. *The Outline of History.* Garden City: Garden City Books, 1961.

Wenham, Gordon J. *Genesis 16–50.* Word Biblical Commentary. Nashville: Nelson, 1994.

———. "Sanctuary Symbolism in the Garden of Eden Story." *Proceedings of the World Jewish Congress of Jewish Studies* 9 (1986) 19–25.

Whybray, R. N. *Introduction to the Pentateuch.* Grand Rapids: Eerdmans, 1995.

———. *The Making of the Pentateuch.* Sheffield: JSOT Press, 1999.

Wilkinson, Bruce. *The Prayer of Jabez: Breaking through to the Blessed Life.* Sisters, OR: Multnomah, 2000.

Wright, Christopher J. H. *Knowing Jesus through the Old Testament.* Downers Grove: InterVarsity, 1992.

Youssef, Michael. *15 Secrets to a Wonderful Life: Mastering the Art of Positive Living.* New York: Faithwords, 2008.

www.ingramcontent.com/pod-product-compliance
Lightning Source LLC
Chambersburg PA
CBHW072154160426
43197CB00012B/2373